TEACHER APPROVED

GET READY
FOR SCHOOL:
PRE-K

485 ACTIVITIES & **2,875** ILLUSTRATIONS

TEACHER APPROVED

GET READY FOR SCHOOL:
PRE-K

HEATHER STELLA

485 ACTIVITIES & **2,875** ILLUSTRATIONS

BLACK DOG
& LEVENTHAL
PUBLISHERS
NEW YORK

Black Dog & Leventhal Publishers
Hachette Book Group
1290 Avenue of the Americas
New York, NY 10104

Distributed in the United Kingdom by Little, Brown Book Group UK, Carmelite House,
50 Victoria Embankment, London, EC4Y 0DZ

www.hachettebookgroup.com
www.blackdogandleventhal.com

Revised & Updated Edition: April 2024

Black Dog & Leventhal Publishers is an imprint of Perseus Books, LLC, a subsidiary of
Hachette Book Group, Inc. The Black Dog & Leventhal Publishers and Get Ready for
School names and logos are trademarks of Hachette Book Group, Inc.

The publisher is not responsible for websites (or their content) that are not owned by
the publisher.

The Hachette Speakers Bureau provides a wide range of authors for speaking
events. To find out more, go to www.hachettespeakersbureau.com or email
HachetteSpeakers@hbgusa.com.

Print book interior design by Clea Chmela

Black Dog & Leventhal books may be purchased in bulk for business, educational, or
promotional use. For more information, please contact your local bookseller or the
Hachette Book Group Special Markets Department at Special.Markets@hbgusa.com.

Library of Congress Control Number: 2023936678

ISBN: 978-0-7624-8324-2 (spiral bound)

Printed in China

APS

10 9 8 7 6 5 4 3 2 1

CONTENTS

A NOTE TO PARENTS

GET READY FOR SCHOOL: PRE-K is an indispensable educational companion for your child about to enter preschool or pre-kindergarten. It is chock-full of fun, interesting, curriculum-based activities—such as those focusing on learning how to write, the alphabet, counting to twenty, colors, shapes, and basic concepts like same, different, opposite, and more—that will introduce your child to learning while reinforcing what they already know. In addition, there are plenty of fun matching games, mazes, and coloring activities that are designed to entertain and amuse your child while boosting their basic skills.

We recommend setting aside some time each day to read with your child. The more your child reads, the faster they will acquire other skills. We also suggest that you have your child complete a portion of the book each day. You and your child can sit down and discuss what the goals for each day will be, and perhaps even choose a reward to be given upon completion of the whole book—such as a trip to the park, a special playdate, or something else that seems appropriate to you.

While you want to help your child set educational goals, be sure to offer lots of encouragement along the way. These activities are not meant as a test. By making these activities fun and rewarding, you will help your child look forward to completing them, ensuring they are eager to tackle the educational challenges ahead!

Hey, kids!
Remember to have
a pencil, some crayons,
stickers, glue, and
Popsicle sticks handy when
playing with your
Get Ready book!

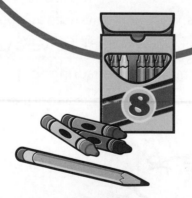

TRACING

Tracing

Trace a line from each dog to its pup.

Now you can write the letter **F**.

Tracing

Trace a line from each cow to its home.

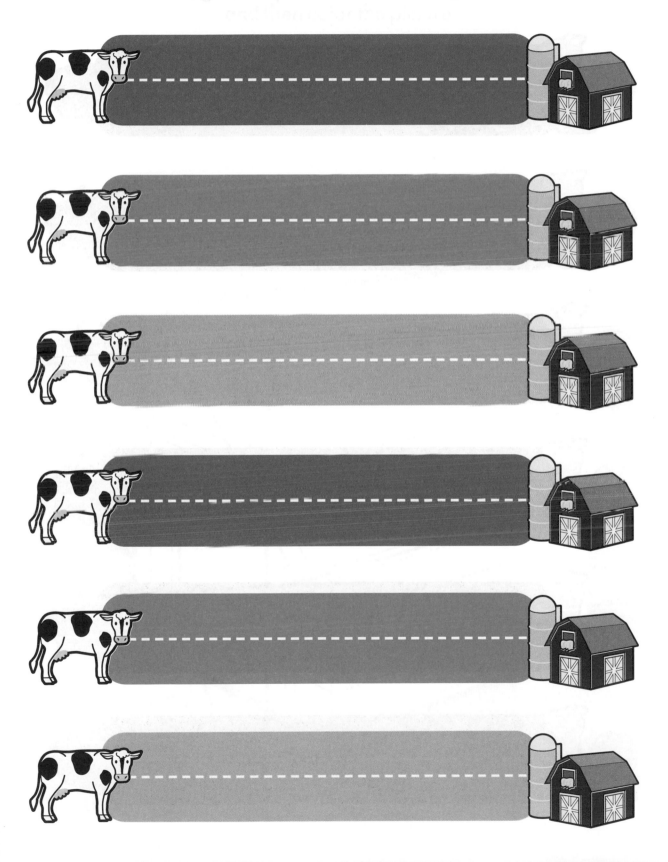

Tracing

Trace a line from each owl to its baby.

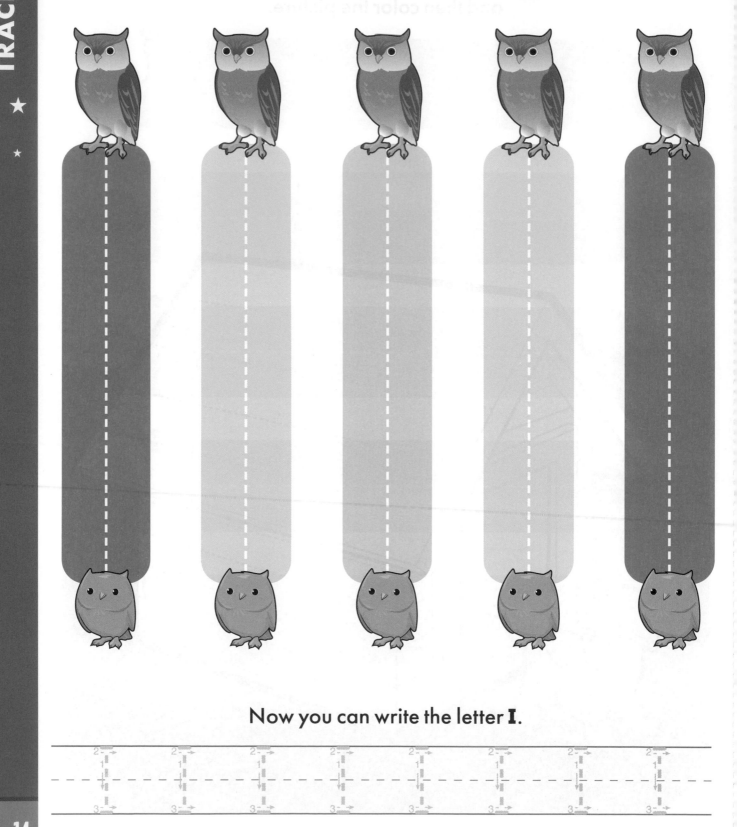

Now you can write the letter **I**.

Tracing

Trace a line from each beaver to its dam.

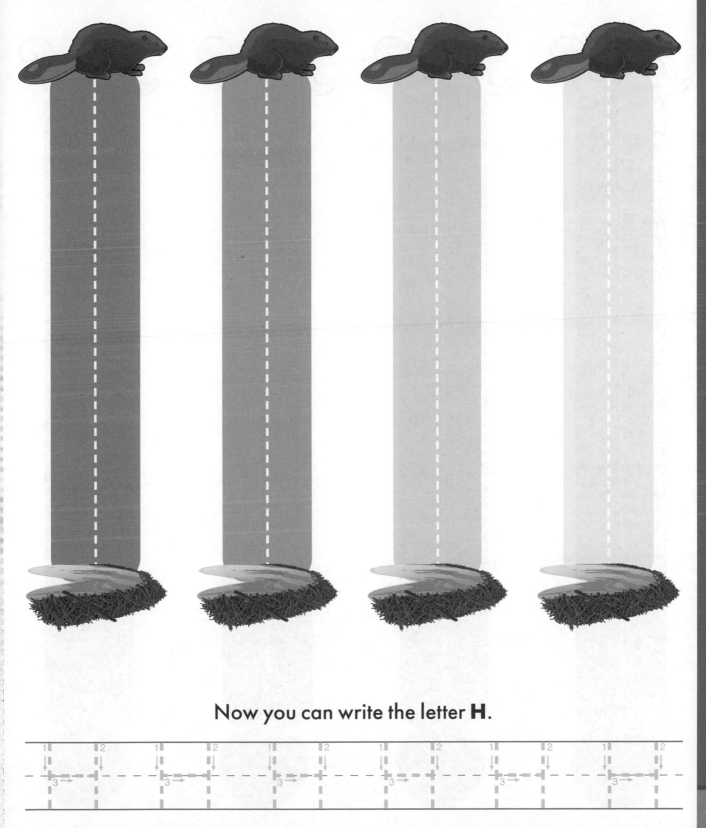

Now you can write the letter **H**.

Tracing

Help each worm find its favorite food by tracing a line to the apple.

Tracing

Trace the dotted lines on the fence and then color the picture.

Trace a line from each pig to its piglet.

Now you can write the letter **V**.

Tracing

Trace a line from each bird to its nest.

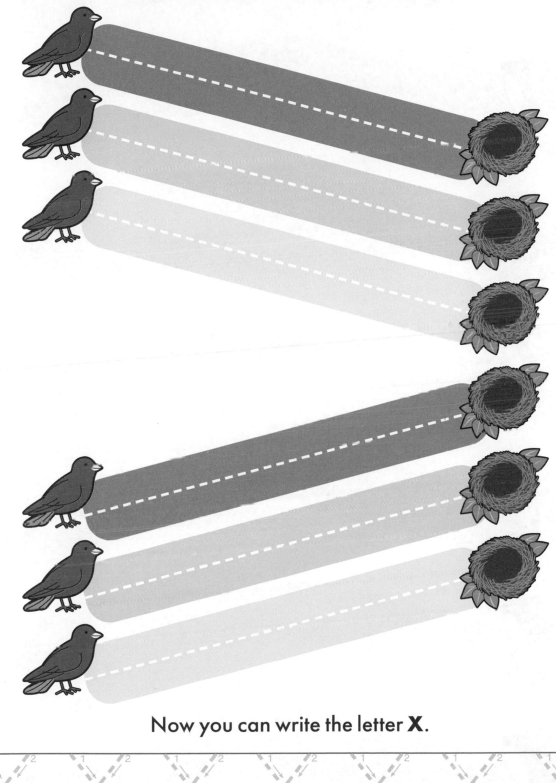

Now you can write the letter **X**.

Help each frog find its favorite food by tracing a line to the fly.

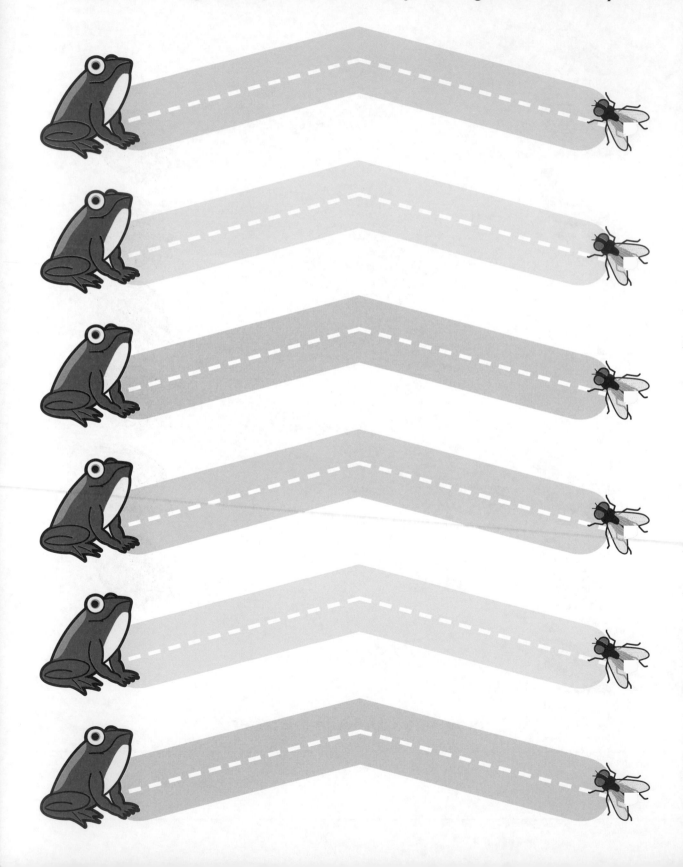

Tracing

Trace the dotted lines on the orange.
Then color the picture.

Tracing

Trace a line from each kangaroo to its baby.

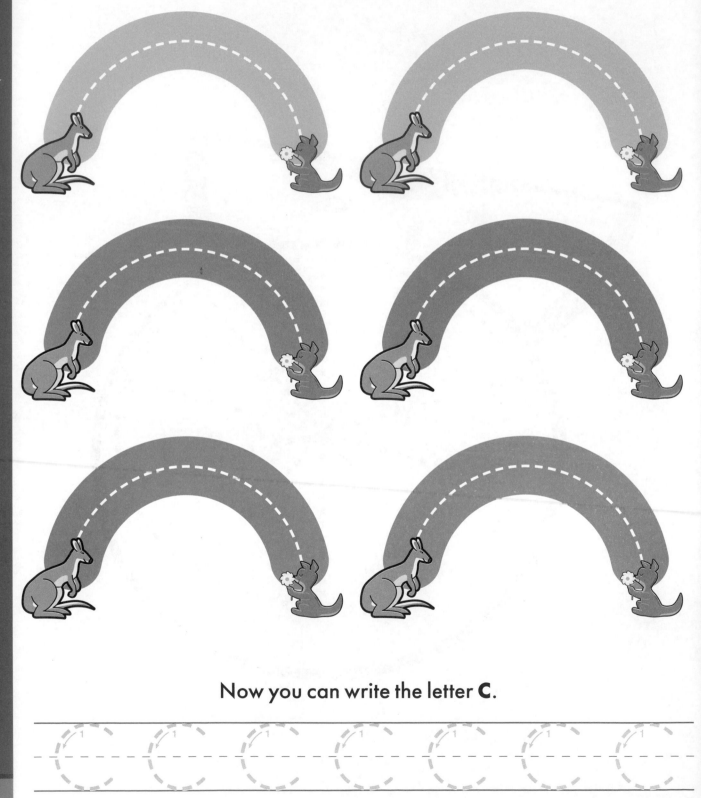

Now you can write the letter **C**.

Trace a line from each dolphin to the ocean.

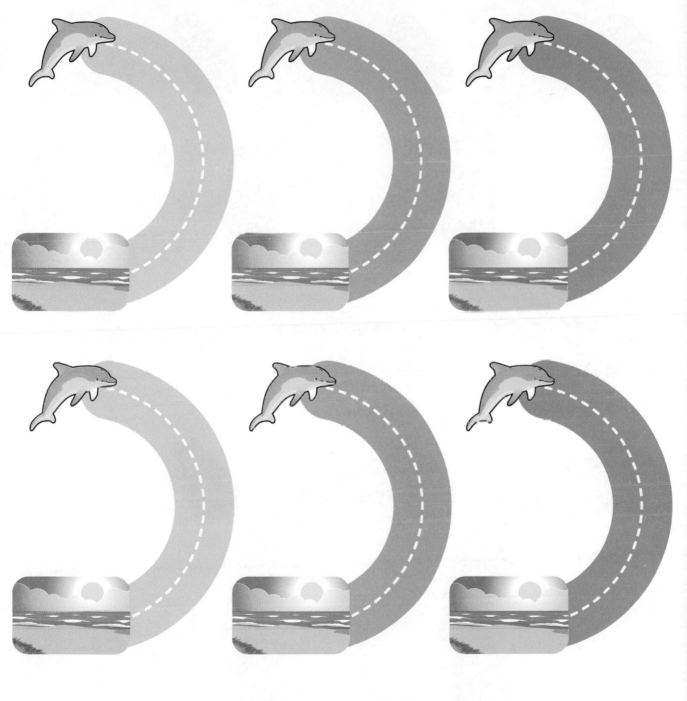

Now you can write the letter **D**.

Trace a line from each bear to its pot of honey.

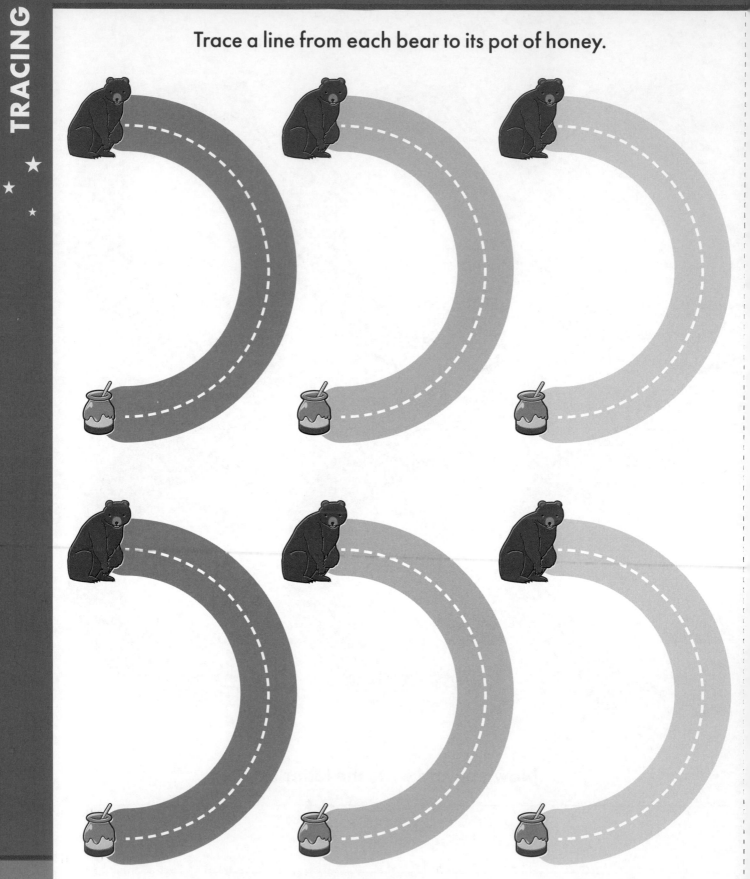

Tracing

Trace the dotted lines on the balloons and then color the picture.

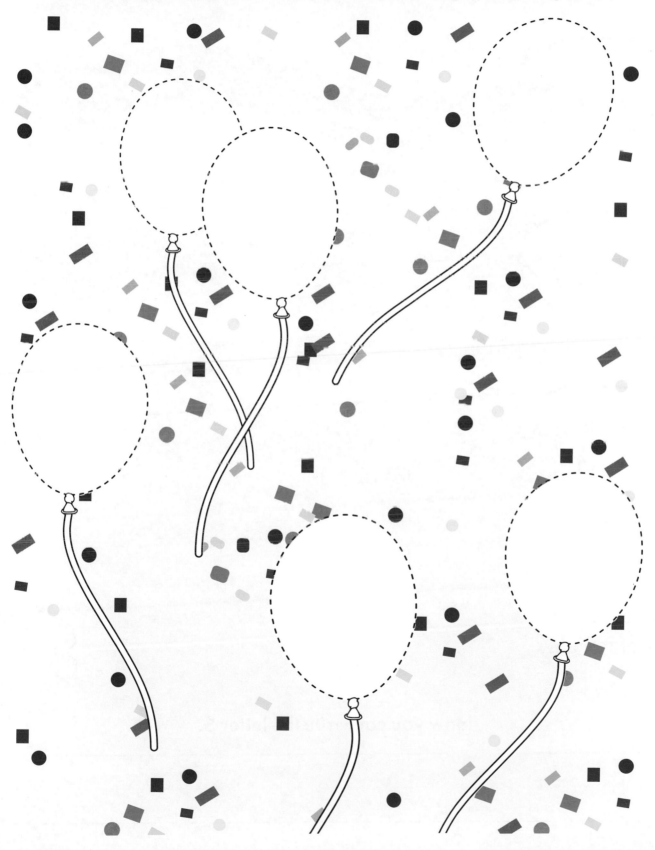

Tracing

Trace a line from each polar bear to its baby.

Now you can write the letter **S**.

Tracing

Trace a line from each spider to its web.

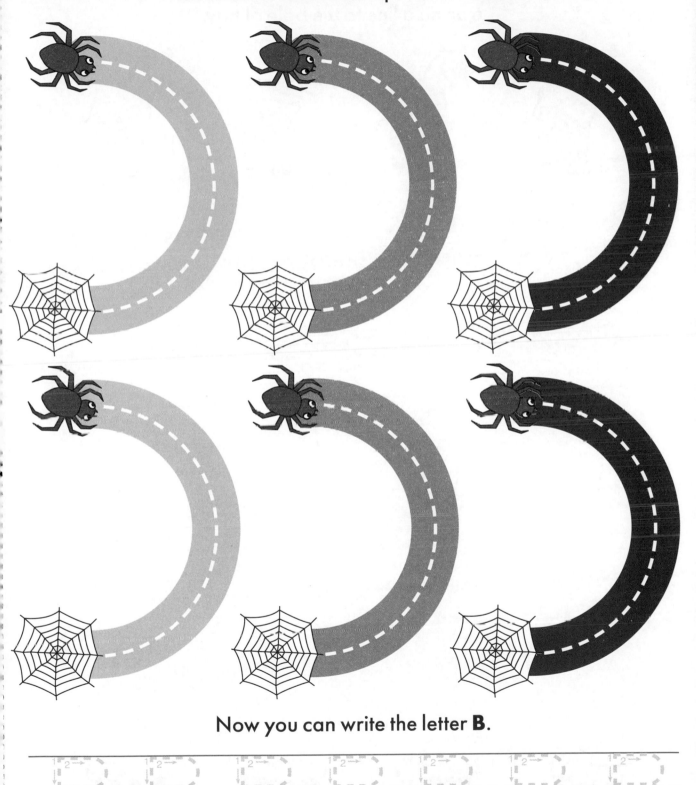

Now you can write the letter **B**.

Tracing

Help each horse find its favorite food by
tracing a line to the bale of hay.

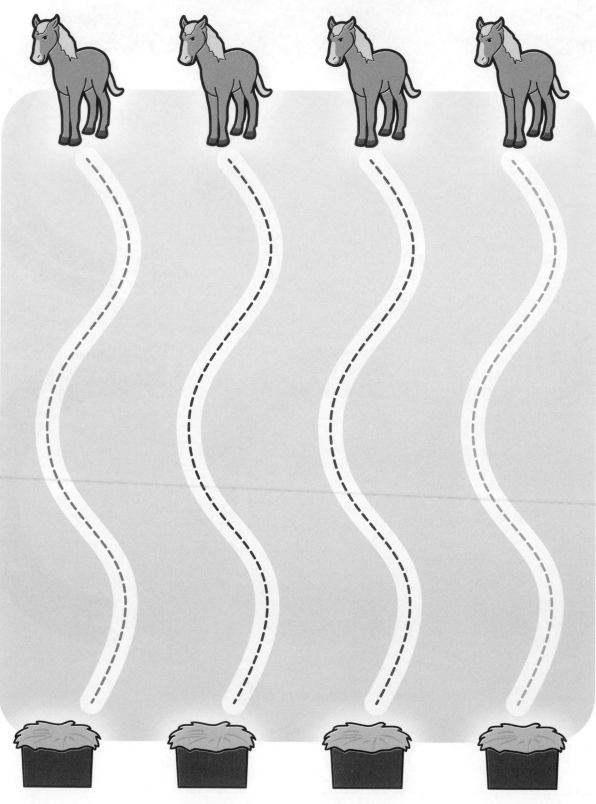

Tracing

Trace the dotted lines on the waves and then color the picture.

Tracing

Trace a line from each elephant to its baby.

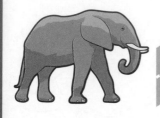

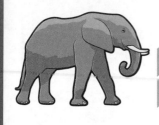

Now you can write the letter **W**.

Trace a line from each chipmunk to its tree.

Now you can write the letter **N**.

Tracing

Trace a line from each toucan to its home.

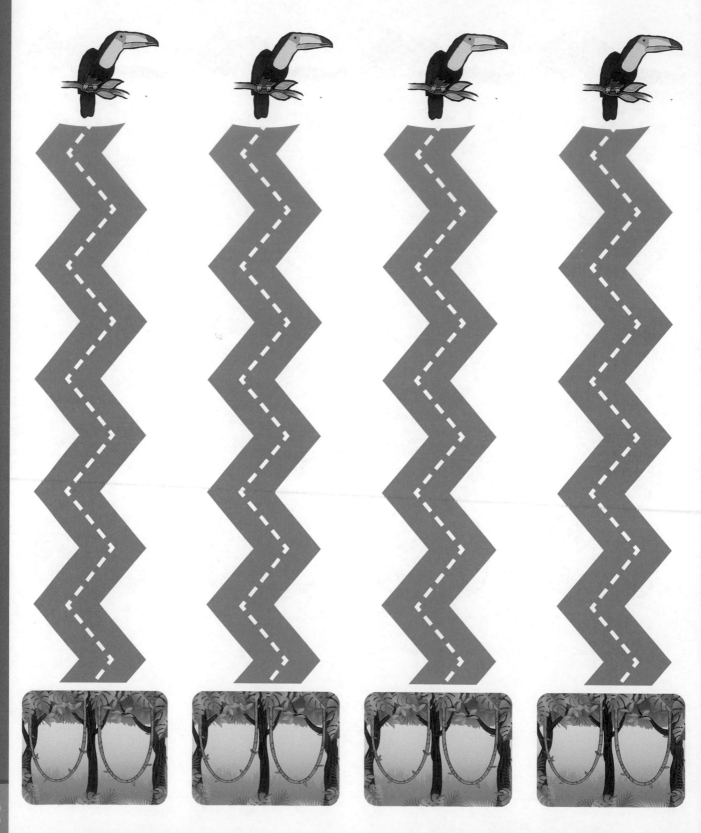

Tracing

Trace the dotted lines on the eggs and then color the picture.

Tracing

Trace a line from each ostrich to its baby.

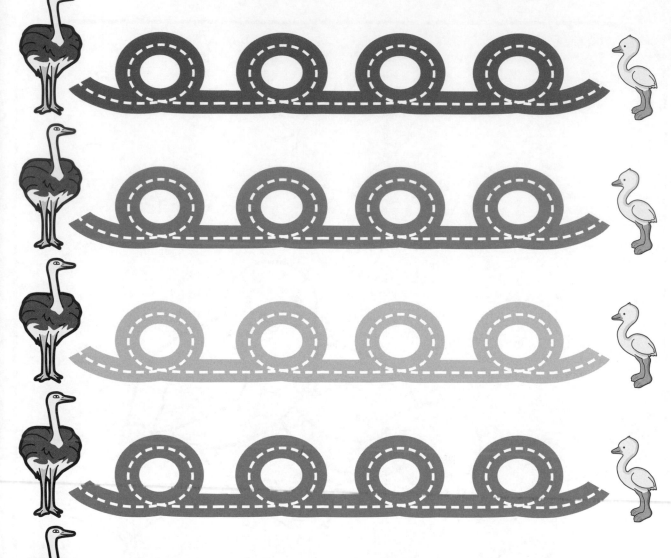

Now you can write the letter O.

Tracing

Trace a line from each seagull to the sky.

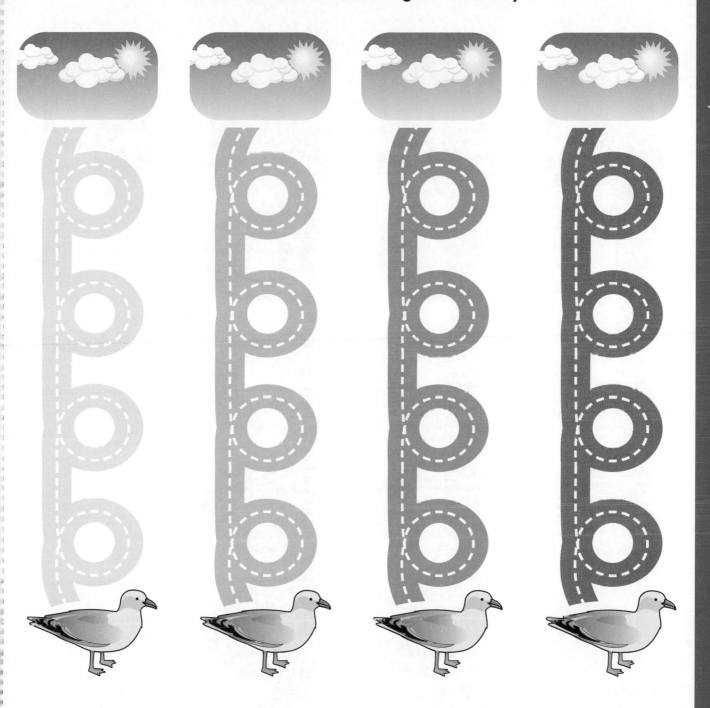

Now you can write the letter **Q**.

Tracing

Trace a line from each gorilla to its favorite food.

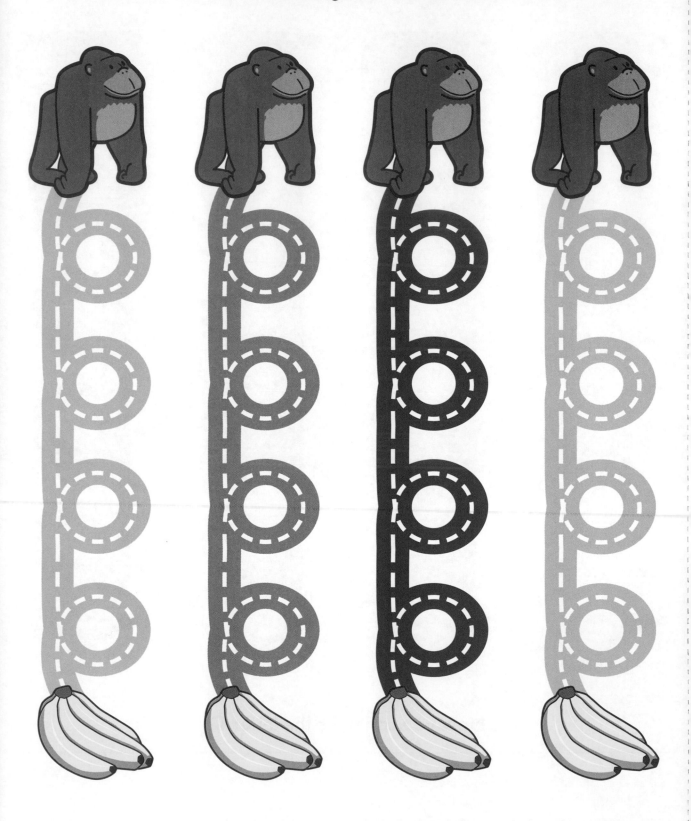

Tracing

Trace the line of each monkey's vine.

Tracing

Trace a line from each chicken to its chick.

Now you can write the letter E.

Tracing

Trace a line from each grasshopper to its home.

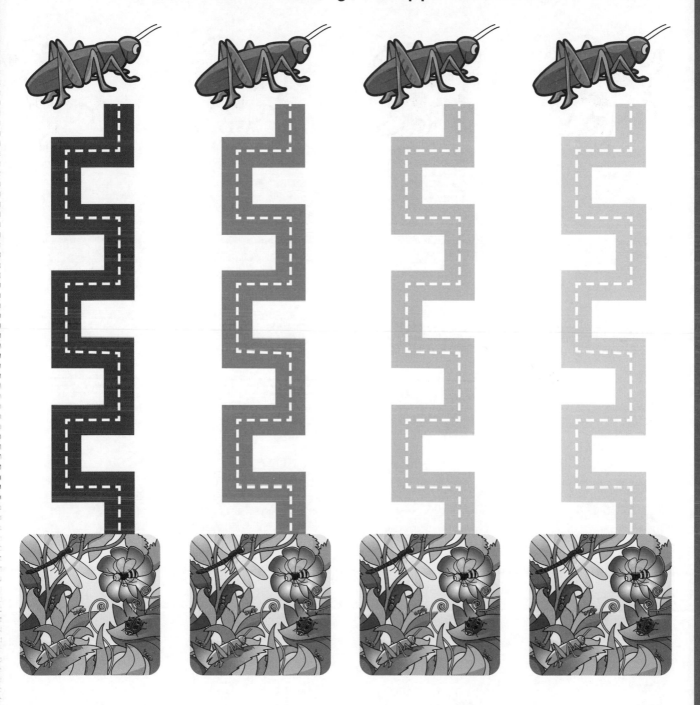

Now you can write the letter **G**.

Tracing

Trace a line from each dog to its favorite food.

ALPHABET

Uppercase Letter A

Trace the uppercase letter **A** with your finger.

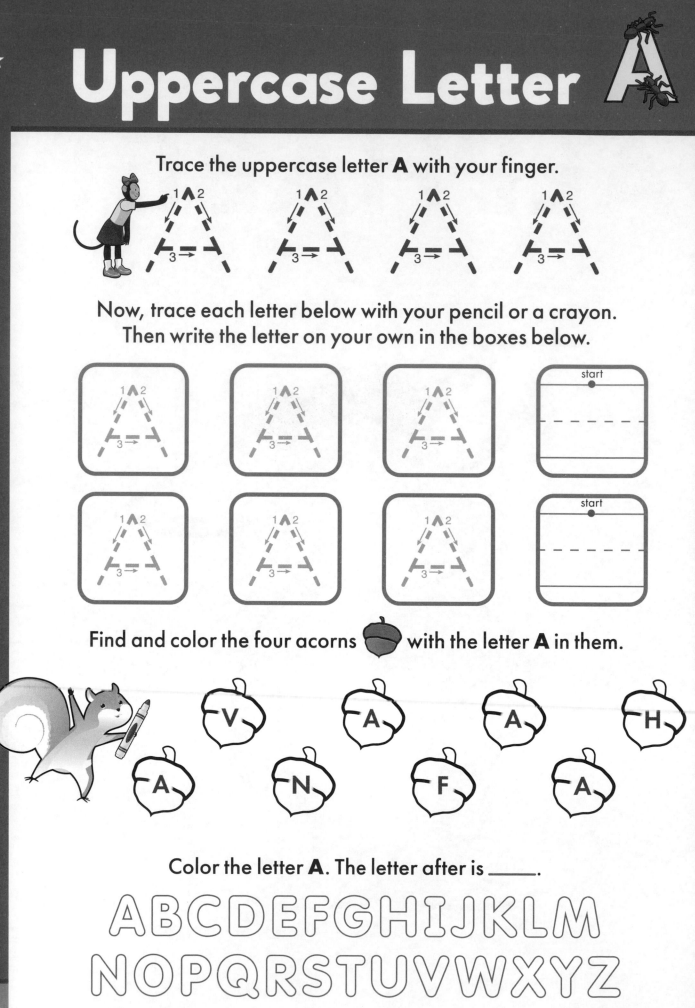

Now, trace each letter below with your pencil or a crayon.
Then write the letter on your own in the boxes below.

start

start

Find and color the four acorns with the letter **A** in them.

V   A   A   H

A   N   F   A

Color the letter **A**. The letter after is _____.

ABCDEFGHIJKLM
NOPQRSTUVWXYZ

Lowercase Letter a

Trace the lowercase letter **a** with your finger.

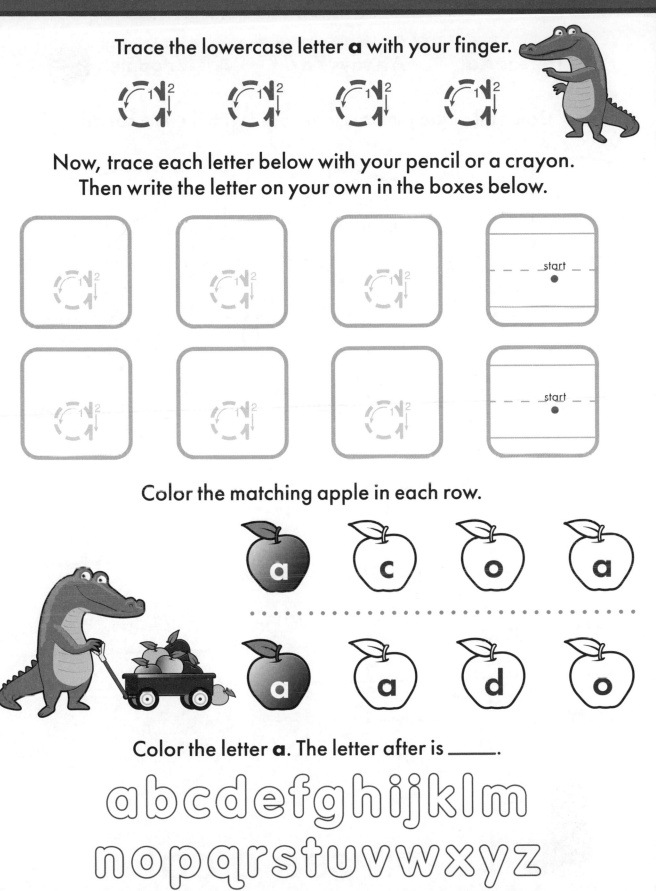

Now, trace each letter below with your pencil or a crayon.
Then write the letter on your own in the boxes below.

start

start

Color the matching apple in each row.

a   c   o   a

a   a   d   o

Color the letter **a**. The letter after is _____.

abcdefghijklm
nopqrstuvwxyz

43

Beginning Sounds

Here is **Aa**.   **Aa** says **/a/**.   **A** is for apple.

Color all of the pictures that begin with the **Aa** sound.

Sight Word

Say the Word	Trace the Word	Circle the Word
can	c a n	can egg cap ant hat can bed jet mop cat can sit

I can see a cat.

Uppercase Letter B

Trace the uppercase letter **B** with your finger.

Now, trace each letter below with your pencil or a crayon.
Then write the letter on your own in the boxes below.

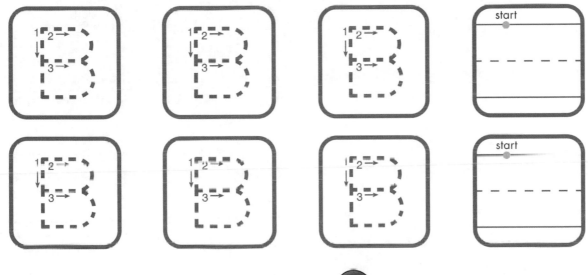

start

start

Find and color the four basketballs ● with the letter **B** in them.

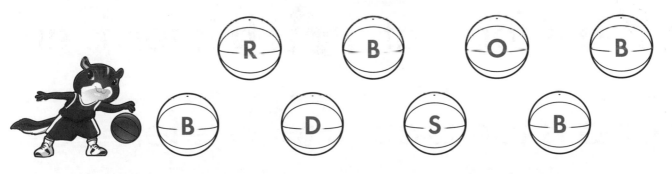

R B O B

B D S B

Color the letter **B**. The letter before is _____. The letter after is _____.

A B C D E F G H I J K L M
N O P Q R S T U V W X Y Z

Lowercase Letter b

Trace the lowercase letter **b** with your finger.

Now, trace each letter below with your pencil or a crayon.
Then write the letter on your own in the boxes below.

start

start

Trace the lowercase letter **b** to complete the word.

b is for **b**at

b is for **b**arn

b is for **b**ed

b is for **b**ee

Color the letter **b**. The letter before is _____. The letter after is _____.

abcdefghijklm
nopqrstuvwxyz

Beginning Sounds

Here is **Bb**.   **Bb** says **/b/**.   **B** is for ball.

Color all of the bubbles with a picture that begins with the **Bb** sound.

Sight Word

Say the Word	Trace the Word	Circle the Word
get		ape by get
		get den pal
		sun so at
		lap get new

Go get the ball.

47

Uppercase Letter C

Trace the uppercase letter **C** with your finger.

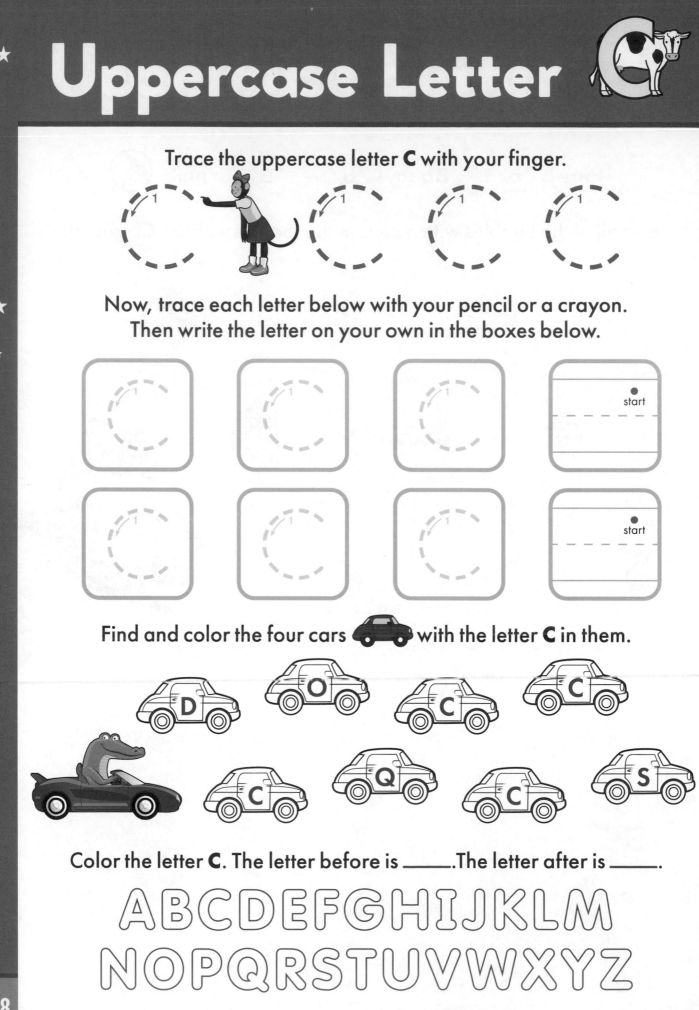

Now, trace each letter below with your pencil or a crayon.
Then write the letter on your own in the boxes below.

start

start

Find and color the four cars with the letter **C** in them.

D

O

C

C

C

Q

C

S

Color the letter **C**. The letter before is _____. The letter after is _____.

ABCDEFGHIJKLM
NOPQRSTUVWXYZ

Lowercase Letter c

Trace the lowercase letter **c** with your finger.

Now, trace each letter below with your pencil or a crayon.
Then write the letter on your own in the boxes below.

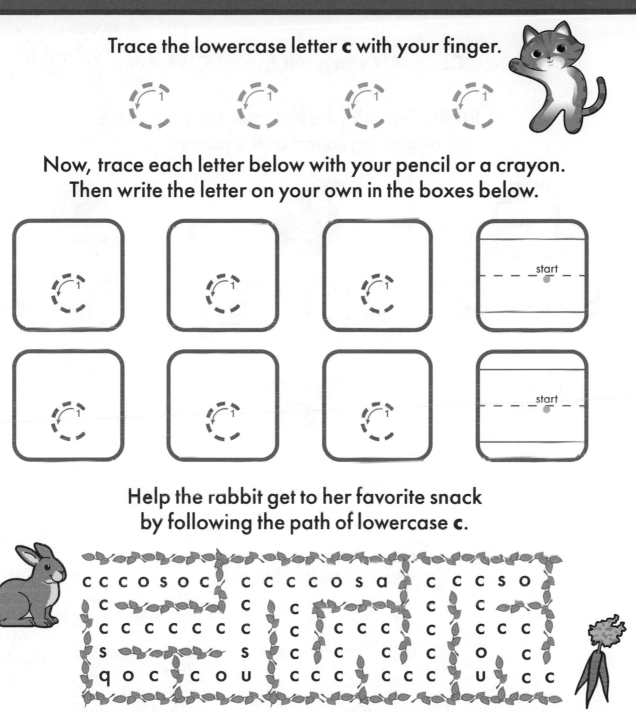

Help the rabbit get to her favorite snack
by following the path of lowercase **c**.

Color the letter **c**. The letter before is _____. The letter after is _____.

abcdefghijklm
nopqrstuvwxyz

Beginning Sounds

Here is **Cc.**   **Cc** says **/k/.**   **C** is for cat.

Color the box with the letter that has the same beginning sound as the picture.

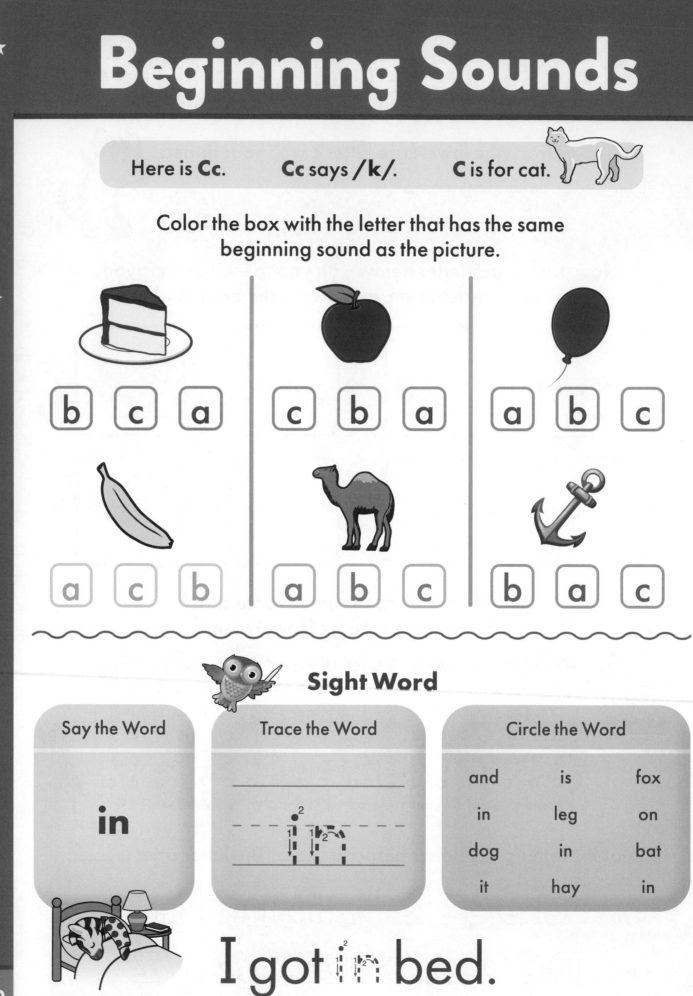

| b | c | a | | c | b | a | | a | b | c |

| a | c | b | | a | b | c | | b | a | c |

Sight Word

Say the Word	Trace the Word	Circle the Word
in		and is fox
		in leg on
		dog in bat
		it hay in

I got in bed.

Trace the uppercase letter **D** with your finger.

Now, trace each letter below with your pencil or a crayon.
Then write the letter on your own in the boxes below.

start

start

Find and color the four dog bones 🦴 with the letter **D** in them.

O   D   P   C

D   G   D   D

Color the letter **D**. The letter before is _____. The letter after is _____.

ABCDEFGHIJKLM
NOPQRSTUVWXYZ

Lowercase Letter d

Trace the lowercase letter **d** with your finger.

Now, trace each letter below with your pencil or a crayon.
Then write the letter on your own in the boxes below.

start

start

Alphabet Soup!

Find and color all lowercase **d**'s.

Color the letter **d**. The letter before is _____. The letter after is _____.

abcdefghijklm
nopqrstuvwxyz

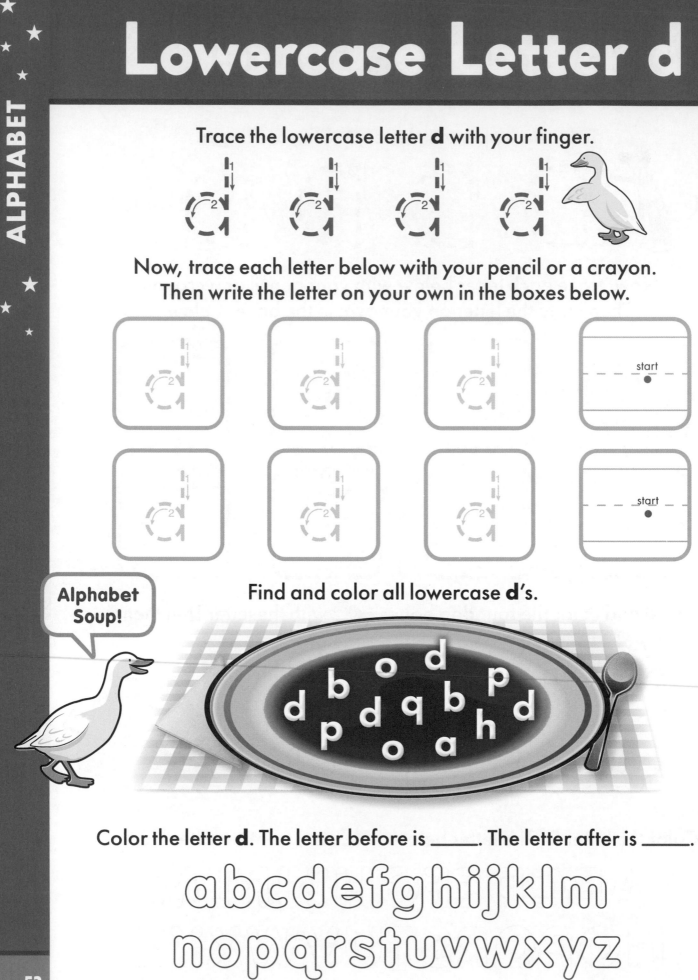

Beginning Sounds

Here is **Dd**.   **Dd** says **/d/**.   **D** is for duck.

Color all of the pictures that begin with the **Dd** sound.

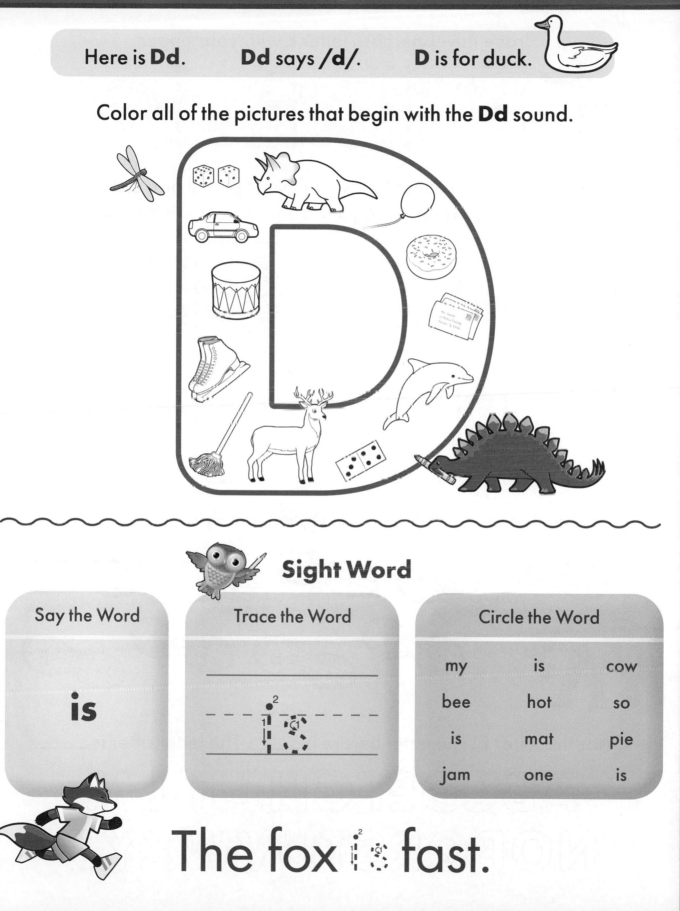

Sight Word

Say the Word	Trace the Word	Circle the Word
is		my is cow
		bee hot so
		is mat pie
		jam one is

The fox is fast.

53

Uppercase Letter

Trace the uppercase letter **E** with your finger.

Now, trace each letter below with your pencil or a crayon.
Then write the letter on your own in the boxes below.

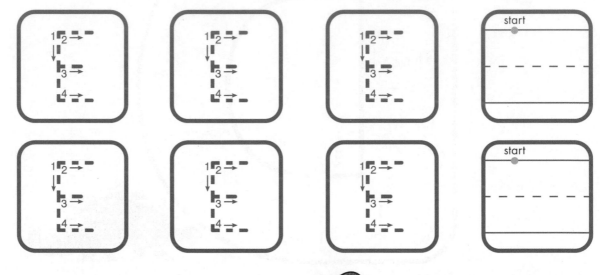

Find and color the four peanuts  with the letter **E** in them.

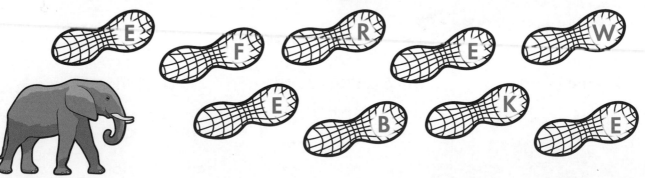

Color the letter **E**. The letter before is _____. The letter after is _____.

ABCDEFGHIJKLM
NOPQRSTUVWXYZ

Lowercase Letter e

Trace the lowercase letter **e** with your finger.

Now, trace each letter below with your pencil or a crayon.
Then write the letter on your own in the boxes below.

start ●

start ●

Find and circle all lowercase **e**'s.

Color the letter **e**. The letter before is _____. The letter after is _____.

abcdefghijklm
nopqrstuvwxyz

55

Beginning Sounds

Here is **Ee**.   **Ee** says **/e/**.   **E** is for eggs.

What animal begins with the letter **Ee**?
Color all of the pictures gray that begin with the **Ee** sound to find out.

Sight Word

Say the Word	Trace the Word	Circle the Word

Say the Word

it

Circle the Word

it	me	bee
air	it	not
dad	let	up
to	it	fur

Is it sunny?

Uppercase Letter F

Trace the uppercase letter **F** with your finger.

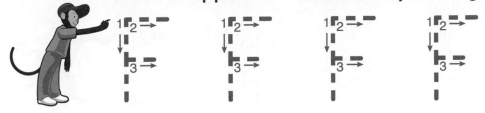

Now, trace each letter below with your pencil or a crayon.
Then write the letter on your own in the boxes below.

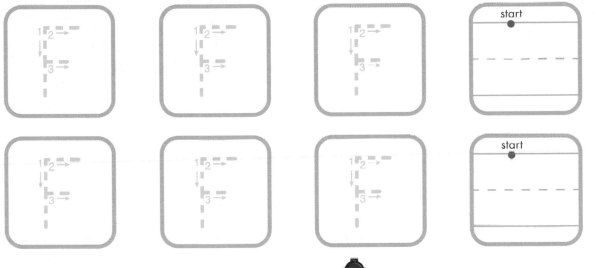

start

start

Find and color the four fire hydrants with the letter **F** in them.

F   T   F   I

J   F   L   F

Color the letter **F**. The letter before is _____. The letter after is _____.

A B C D E F G H I J K L M
N O P Q R S T U V W X Y Z

Lowercase Letter f

Trace the lowercase letter **f** with your finger.

Now, trace each letter below with your pencil or a crayon.
Then write the letter on your own in the boxes below.

start

start

Help the farmer get to his farm by following the path of lowercase **f**.

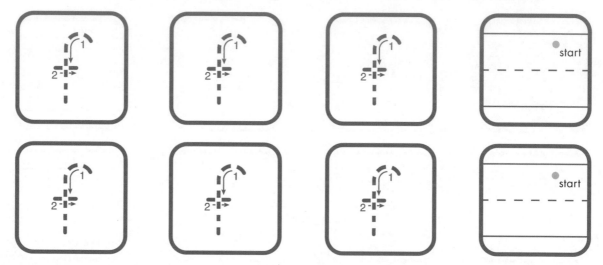

Color the letter **f**. The letter before is _____. The letter after is _____.

abcdefghijklm
nopqrstuvwxyz

Beginning Sounds

Here is **Ff**.   **Ff** says **/f/**.   **F** is for frog.

Color the box with the letter that has the same beginning sound as the picture.

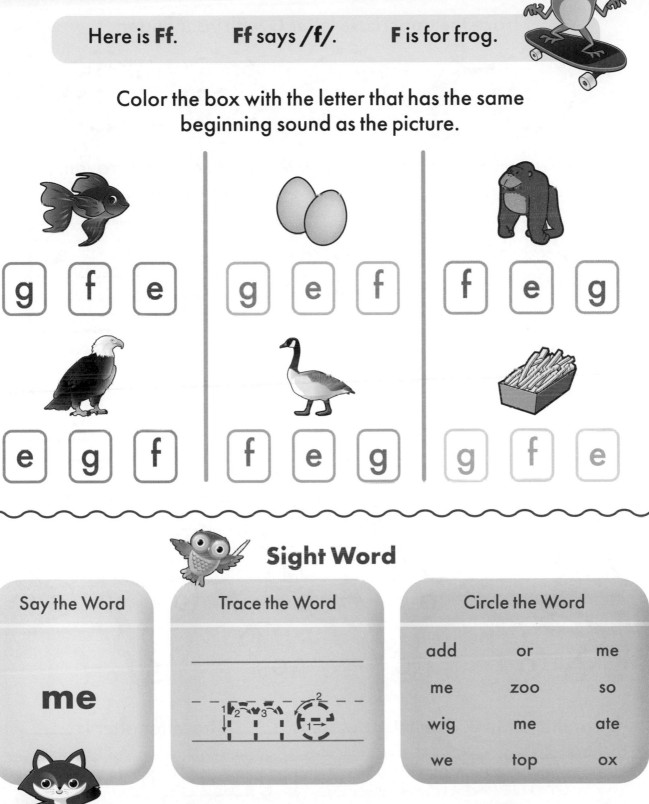

| g | f | e | | g | e | f | | f | e | g |

| e | g | f | | f | e | g | | g | f | e |

Sight Word

Say the Word	Trace the Word	Circle the Word
me	me	add or me me zoo so wig me ate we top ox

Will you play with me?

Uppercase Letter G

Trace the uppercase letter **G** with your finger.

Now, trace each letter below with your pencil or a crayon.
Then write the letter on your own in the boxes below.

start

start

Find and color the four guitars with the letter **G** in them.

O   G   G   Q   G   D   C   G

Color the letter **G**. The letter before is _____. The letter after is _____.

ABCDEFGHIJKLM
NOPQRSTUVWXYZ

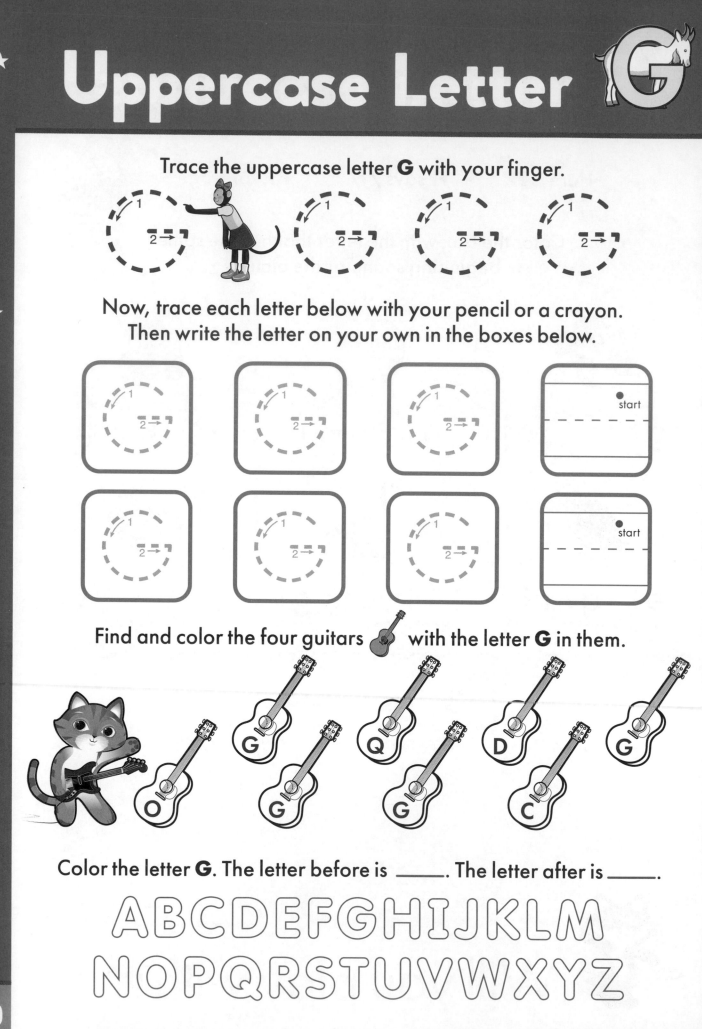

Trace the lowercase letter **g** with your finger.

Now, trace each letter below with your pencil or a crayon.
Then write the letter on your own in the boxes below.

• start

• start

Find and color all lowercase **g**'s.

Alphabet Soup!

Color the letter **g**. The letter before is _____. The letter after is _____.

abcdefghijklm
nopqrstuvwxyz

Beginning Sounds

Here is **Gg**.   **Gg** says **/g/**.   **G** is for grapes.

Color all of the pictures that begin with the **Gg** sound.

Sight Word

Say the Word	Trace the Word	Circle the Word

see

dim   aid   see

see   ivy   if

hit   see   lad

am   mom   be

I see a dog.

Uppercase Letter H

Trace the uppercase letter **H** with your finger.

Now, trace each letter below with your pencil or a crayon.
Then write the letter on your own in the boxes below.

start

start

Find and color the four hamburgers with the letter **H** in them.

| H | F | H | H |
| H | K | N | Z |

Color the letter **H**. The letter before is _____. The letter after is _____.

ABCDEFGHIJKLM
NOPQRSTUVWXYZ

Lowercase Letter h

Trace the lowercase letter **h** with your finger.

Now, trace each letter below with your pencil or a crayon.
Then write the letter on your own in the boxes below.

start

start

Trace the lowercase letter **h** to complete the word.

h is for **h**orse

h is for **h**eart

h is for **h**og

h is for **h**at

Color the letter **h**. The letter before is _____. The letter after is _____.

abcdefghijklm
nopqrstuvwxyz

Beginning Sounds

Here is **Hh**.   **Hh** says **/h/**.   **H** is for hat.

Color all of the hearts with a picture
that begins with the **Hh** sound.

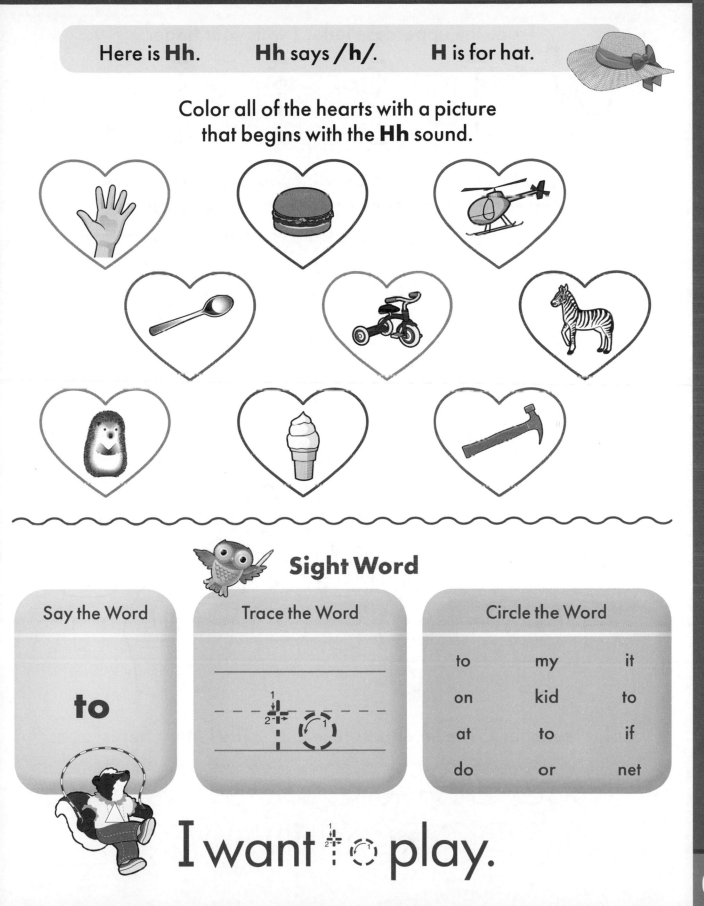

Sight Word

Say the Word	Trace the Word	Circle the Word
to		to my it
		on kid to
		at to if
		do or net

I want to play.

65

Uppercase Letter I

Trace the uppercase letter **I** with your finger.

Now, trace each letter below with your pencil or a crayon.
Then write the letter on your own in the boxes below.

start

start

Find and color the four ice-cream cones with the letter **I** in them.

I   L   J   I   F   T   I   L   I

Color the letter **I**. The letter before is _____. The letter after is _____.

ABCDEFGHIJKLM
NOPQRSTUVWXYZ

Lowercase Letter i

Trace the lowercase letter **i** with your finger.

Now, trace each letter below with your pencil or a crayon.
Then write the letter on your own in the boxes below.

start

start

Tic-Tac-Toe!

Find three words in a row that begin with the letter **i**.
You can go across, down, or diagonal. Circle the letter **i**'s.

it	is	in
at	do	so
no	if	go

do	is	in
go	it	no
if	so	at

so	do	it
no	is	in
go	at	if

Color the letter **i**. The letter before is _____. The letter after is _____.

abcdefghijklm
nopqrstuvwxyz

67

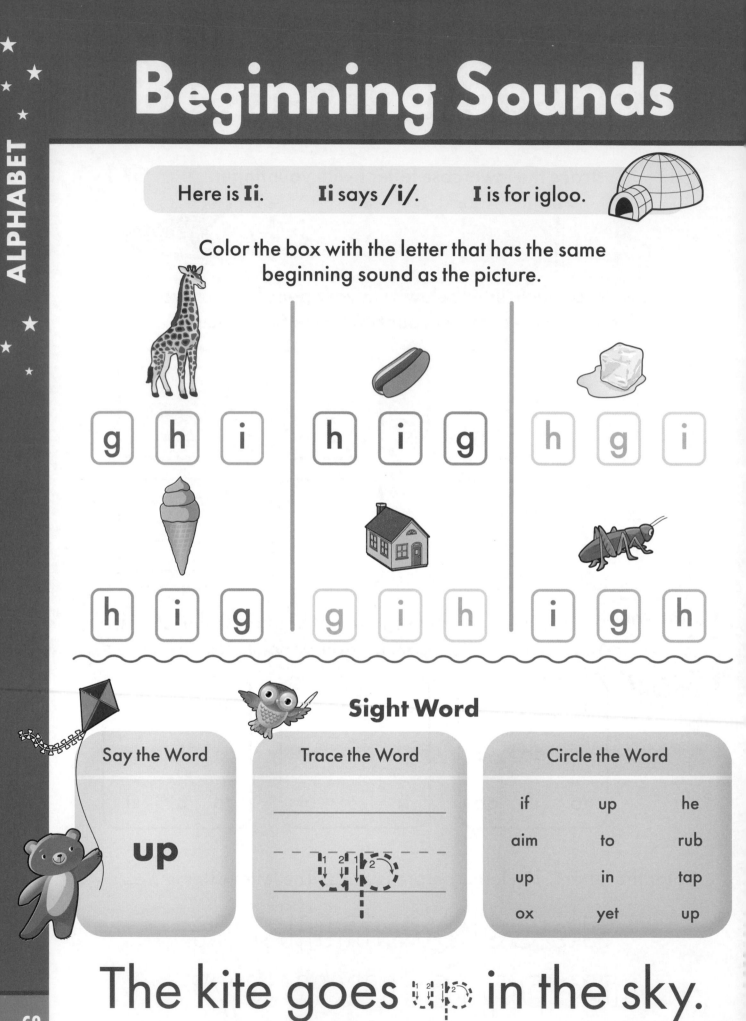

Beginning Sounds

ALPHABET

Here is **Ii**.   **Ii** says **/i/**.   **I** is for igloo.

Color the box with the letter that has the same beginning sound as the picture.

g	h	i		h	i	g		h	g	i

h	i	g		g	i	h		i	g	h

Sight Word

Say the Word	Trace the Word	Circle the Word
up		if up he
		aim to rub
		up in tap
		ox yet up

The kite goes up in the sky.

68

Uppercase Letter

Trace the uppercase letter **J** with your finger.

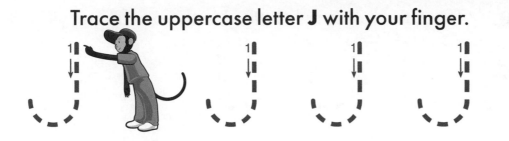

Now, trace each letter below with your pencil or a crayon.
Then write the letter on your own in the boxes below.

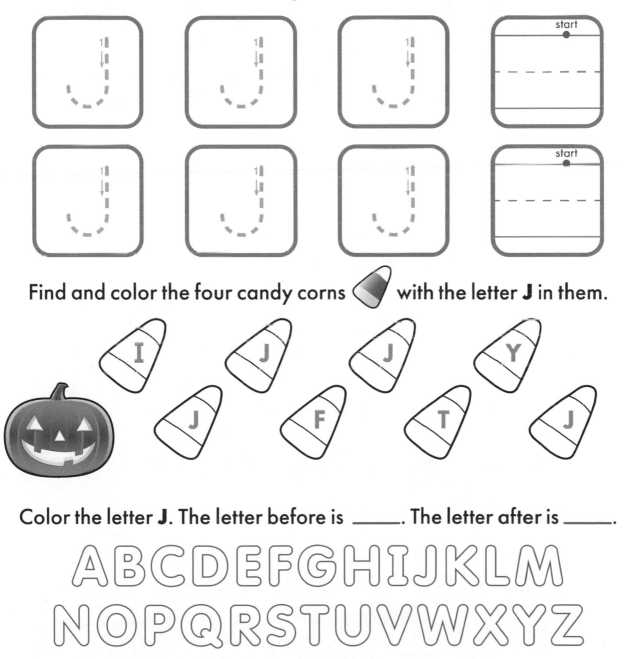

start

start

Find and color the four candy corns with the letter **J** in them.

I   J   J   Y

J   F   T   J

Color the letter **J**. The letter before is ____. The letter after is ____.

ABCDEFGHIJKLM
NOPQRSTUVWXYZ

Lowercase Letter j

Trace the lowercase letter **j** with your finger.

Now, trace each letter below with your pencil or a crayon.
Then write the letter on your own in the boxes below.

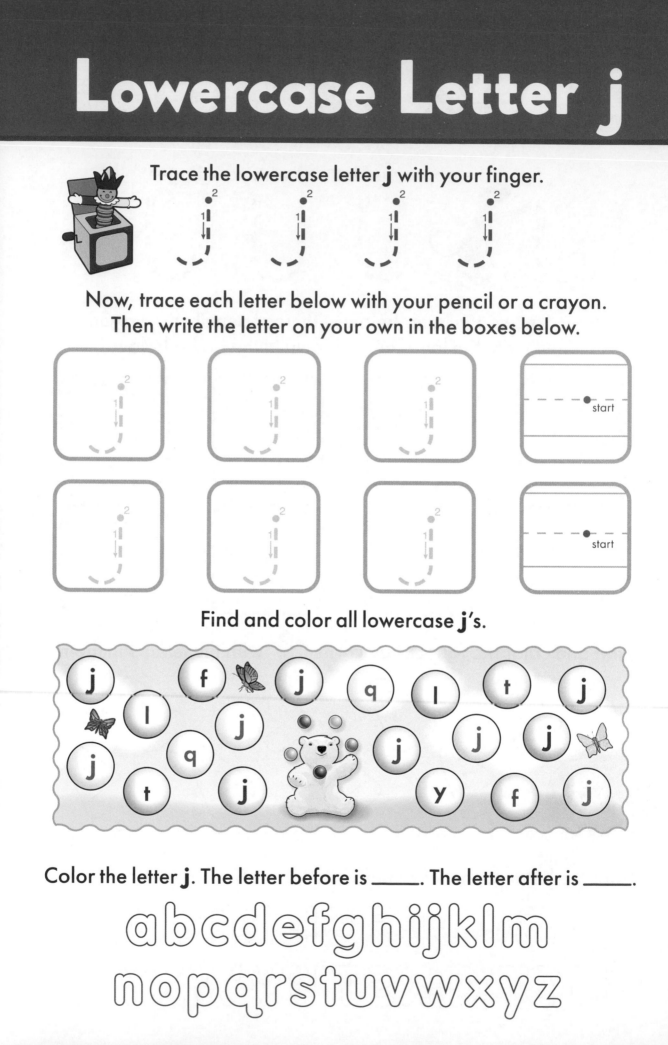

Find and color all lowercase **j**'s.

Color the letter **j**. The letter before is _____. The letter after is _____.

abcdefghijklm
nopqrstuvwxyz

Beginning Sounds

Here is **J j**.   **J j** says **/j/**.   **J** is for jar.

Help Brian the Bunny pack his backpack.
Circle the pictures of clothing that begin with the **J j** sound.

Sight Word

Say the Word	Trace the Word	Circle the Word
we		

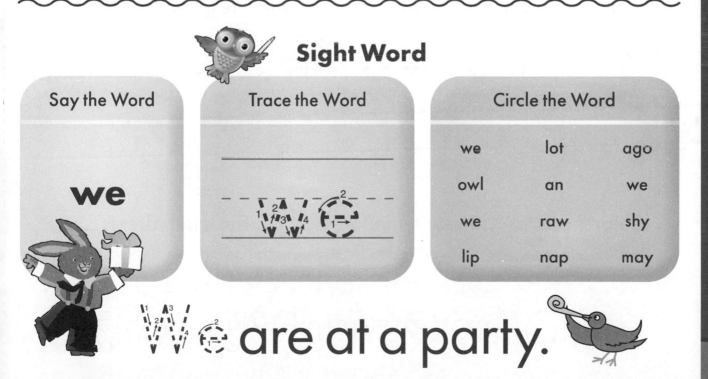

Circle the Word:

we	lot	ago
owl	an	we
we	raw	shy
lip	nap	may

We are at a party.

71

Uppercase Letter

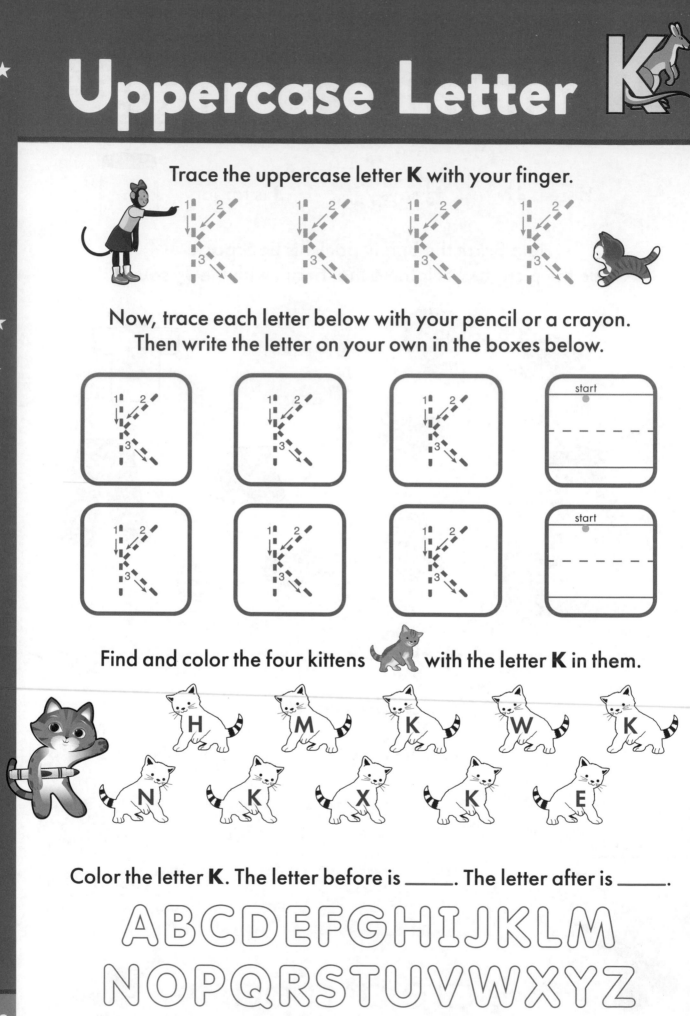

Trace the uppercase letter **K** with your finger.

Now, trace each letter below with your pencil or a crayon.
Then write the letter on your own in the boxes below.

start

start

Find and color the four kittens with the letter **K** in them.

H   M   K   W   K

N   K   X   K   E

Color the letter **K**. The letter before is _____. The letter after is _____.

ABCDEFGHIJKLM
NOPQRSTUVWXYZ

Trace the lowercase letter **k** with your finger.

Now, trace each letter below with your pencil or a crayon.
Then write the letter on your own in the boxes below.

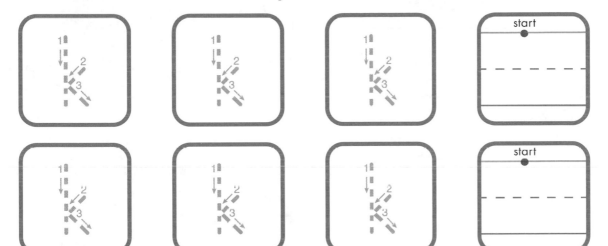

start

start

Find and circle all the lowercase **k**'s.

k   f   h   k   k   k   l
    h   y   k   z
w t   h   k   x   h   y
        l   f
        k   y   h   k
x   f   l   k   k

Color the letter **k**. The letter before is _____. The letter after is _____.

abcdefghijklm
nopqrstuvwxyz

Beginning Sounds

Here is **Kk**.   **Kk** says **/k/**.   **K** is for kite.

Color all of the pictures that begin with the **Kk** sound.

Sight Word

Say the Word	Trace the Word	Circle the Word

you

ax	you	new
low	hot	paw
pet	go	you
you	sun	egg

I love you.

Uppercase Letter

Trace the uppercase letter **L** with your finger.

Now, trace each letter below with your pencil or a crayon.
Then write the letter on your own in the boxes below.

start

start

Find and color the six leaves with the letter **L** in them.

J   L   E   J   L

F   T   V

L   L   L   K

Color the letter **L**. The letter before is _____. The letter after is _____.

ABCDEFGHIJKLM
NOPQRSTUVWXYZ

Lowercase Letter l

Trace the lowercase letter **l** with your finger.

Now, trace each letter below with your pencil or a crayon.
Then write the letter on your own in the boxes below.

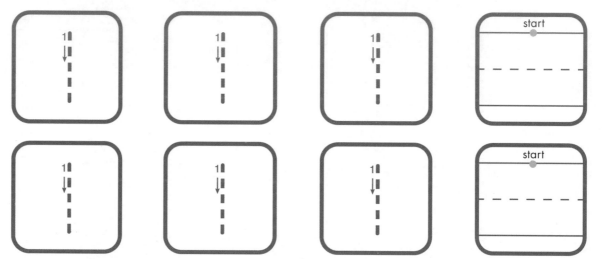

start

start

Help the frog get to its lily pad by following the path of lowercase **l**.

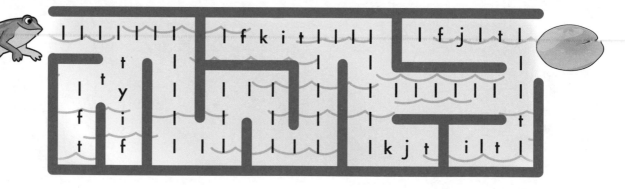

Color the letter **l**. The letter before is _____. The letter after is _____.

abcdefghijklm
nopqrstuvwxyz

Beginning Sounds

Here is **Ll**. **Ll** says /l/. **L** is for lion.

Color the box with the letter that has the same beginning sound as the picture.

k	l	j		l	k	j		j	k	l

k	j	l		j	k	l		j	l	k

Sight Word

Say the Word	Trace the Word	Circle the Word
the		the pad ago
		tad the raw
		sow own tin
		ran the nab

The pig is dirty.

Uppercase Letter M

Trace the uppercase letter **M** with your finger.

Now, trace each letter below with your pencil or a crayon.
Then write the letter on your own in the boxes below.

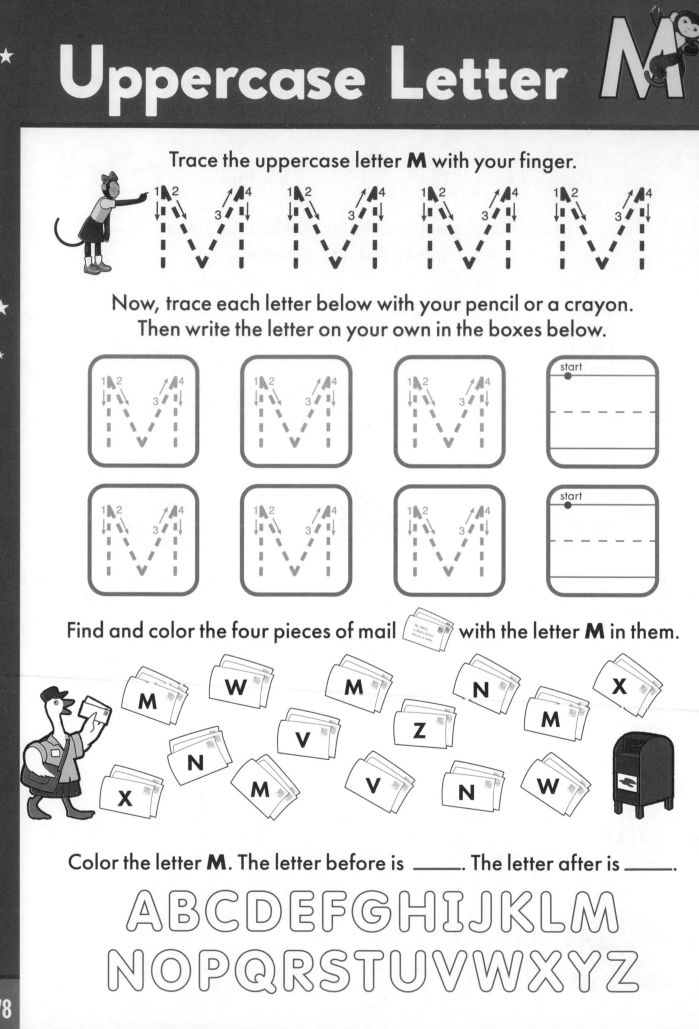

start

start

Find and color the four pieces of mail with the letter **M** in them.

M   W   M   N   X

N   V   Z   M

X   M   V   N   W

Color the letter **M**. The letter before is _____. The letter after is _____.

ABCDEFGHIJKLM
NOPQRSTUVWXYZ

Lowercase Letter m

Trace the lowercase letter **m** with your finger.

1 2 3 m   1 2 3 m   1 2 3 m   1 2 3 m

Now, trace each letter below with your pencil or a crayon.
Then write the letter on your own in the boxes below.

start

start

Help the monkey find its way through the jungle
by following the path of lowercase **m**.

m	n	e	w	m	n	r	m	w		m	m	m	m	n	v	h	m
m								m			m			m			n
m	m	m	m	m	m			w		n		m	m	n			v
n					m		m			h			m	n			x
w	m	n	v	m	n		m	m	m	m			m		k		c
o				m			m		m	v		m		n			
c	m	w	v	n	m	u	v	m		n	w		m	m	m	→	

Color the letter **m**. The letter before is _____. The letter after is _____.

abcdefghijklm
nopqrstuvwxyz

79

Beginning Sounds

Here is **Mm**.   **Mm** says **/m/**.   **M** is for mop.

Color all of the pictures that begin with the **Mm** sound.

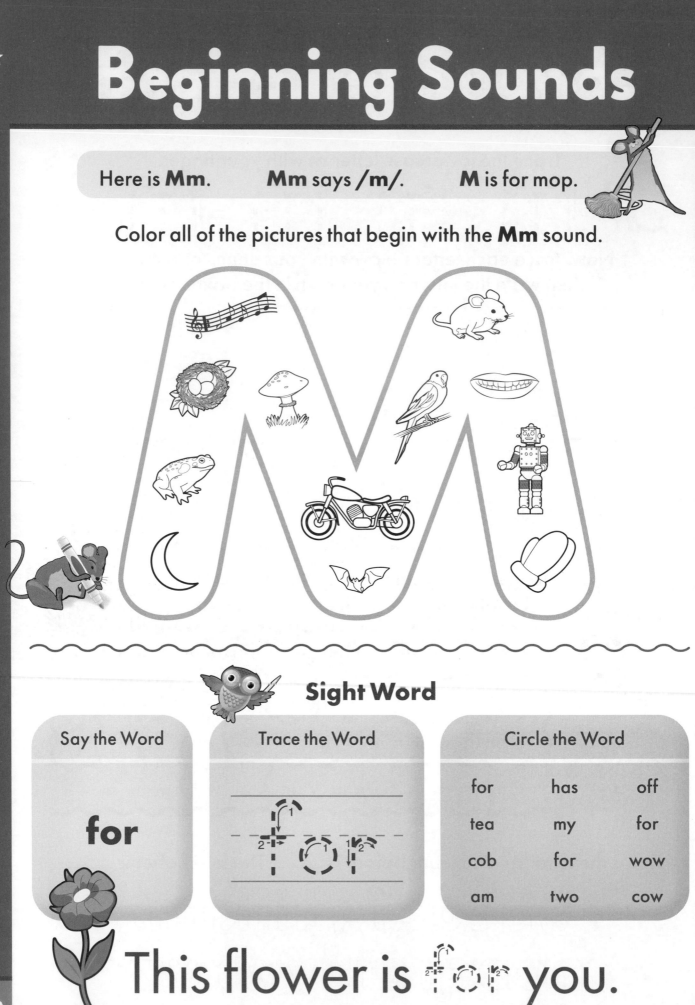

Sight Word

Say the Word	Trace the Word	Circle the Word
for		

Circle the Word:

for	has	off
tea	my	for
cob	for	wow
am	two	cow

This flower is for you.

Uppercase Letter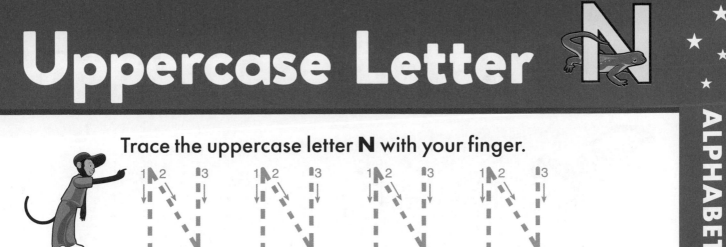

Trace the uppercase letter **N** with your finger.

Now, trace each letter below with your pencil or a crayon.
Then write the letter on your own in the boxes below.

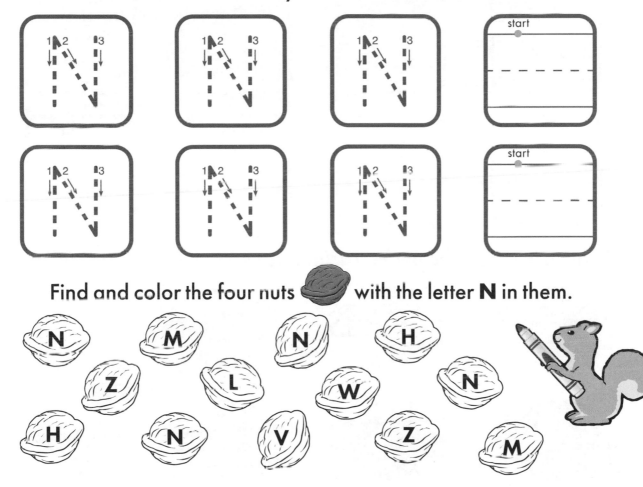

Find and color the four nuts with the letter **N** in them.

Color the letter **N**. The letter before is _____. The letter after is _____.

ABCDEFGHIJKLM
NOPQRSTUVWXYZ

Lowercase Letter n

Trace the lowercase letter **n** with your finger.

Now, trace each letter below with your pencil or a crayon. Then write the letter on your own in the boxes below.

start

start

Draw a line from the uppercase nest to its matching lowercase nest.

M   N   W

w   m   n

Color the letter **n**. The letter before is _____. The letter after is _____.

abcdefghijklm
nopqrstuvwxyz

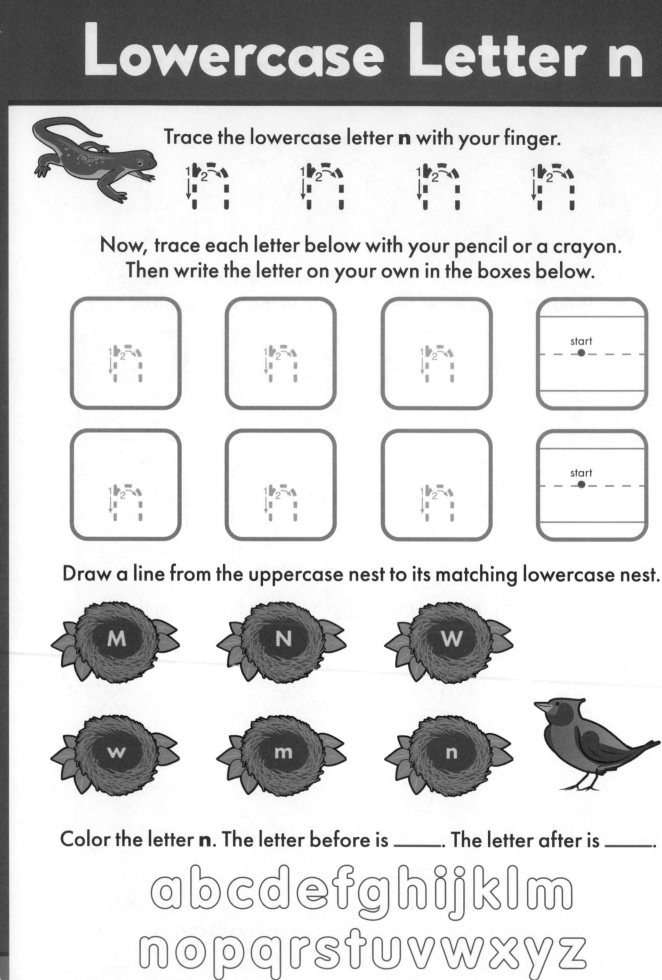

Beginning Sounds

Here is **Nn**. **Nn** says **/n/**. **N** is for nose.

Color all of the pictures that begin with the **Nn** sound.

Sight Word

Say the Word	Trace the Word	Circle the Word
big		an tow act big end he jar big oil big met oh

I see a big truck.

83

Uppercase Letter

Trace the uppercase letter **O** with your finger.

Now, trace each letter below with your pencil or a crayon.
Then write the letter on your own in the boxes below.

start

start

Find and color the four octopuses  with the letter **O** in them.

Color the letter **O**. The letter before is _____. The letter after is _____.

ABCDEFGHIJKLM
NOPQRSTUVWXYZ

Lowercase Letter o

Trace the lowercase letter o with your finger.

Now, trace each letter below with your pencil or a crayon.
Then write the letter on your own in the boxes below.

start

start

Find and circle all lowercase o's.

o
d
c
b
e
p
p
e
c
p
p
o
e
d
p
c
q
g
o
d
b
e
c
g
b
d
o
e
b
o
e
o
g
o
c
o
b
c
o
q
c
p

Color the letter o. The letter before is _____. The letter after is _____.

abcdefghijklm
nopqrstuvwxyz

85

Beginning Sounds

Here is **Oo**.   **Oo** says /**o**/.   **O** is for octopus.

Color all of the pictures that begin with the **Oo** sound.

Sight Word

Say the Word

not

Trace the Word

Circle the Word

be	err	not
urn	nut	ink
get	ax	not
not	sit	do

I am not happy.

Trace the uppercase letter **P** with your finger.

P P P P

Now, trace each letter below with your pencil or a crayon.
Then write the letter on your own in the boxes below.

P P P

start

P P P

start

Find and color the four party hats with the letter **P** in them.

P C Q P D
B D R
R D P B P

Color the letter **P**. The letter before is _____. The letter after is _____.

ABCDEFGHIJKLM
NOPQRSTUVWXYZ

Lowercase Letter p

Trace the lowercase letter **p** with your finger.

Now, trace each letter below with your pencil or a crayon.
Then write the letter on your own in the boxes below.

start

start

Trace the lowercase **p** to complete the word.

p is for pear

p is for peas

p is for pig

p is for pencil

Color the letter **p**. The letter before is _____. The letter after is _____.

abcdefghijklm
nopqrstuvwxyz

Beginning Sounds

Here is **Pp**.   **Pp** says /p/.   **P** is for panda.

Color the box with the letter that has the same beginning sound as the picture.

o	n	p

p	o	n

n	p	o

p	n	o

p	n	o

n	o	p

Sight Word

Say the Word	Trace the Word	Circle the Word
one	one	ah one ore hum pig as nip one mat in fog one

I see one bird.

Uppercase Letter Q

Trace the uppercase letter **Q** with your finger.

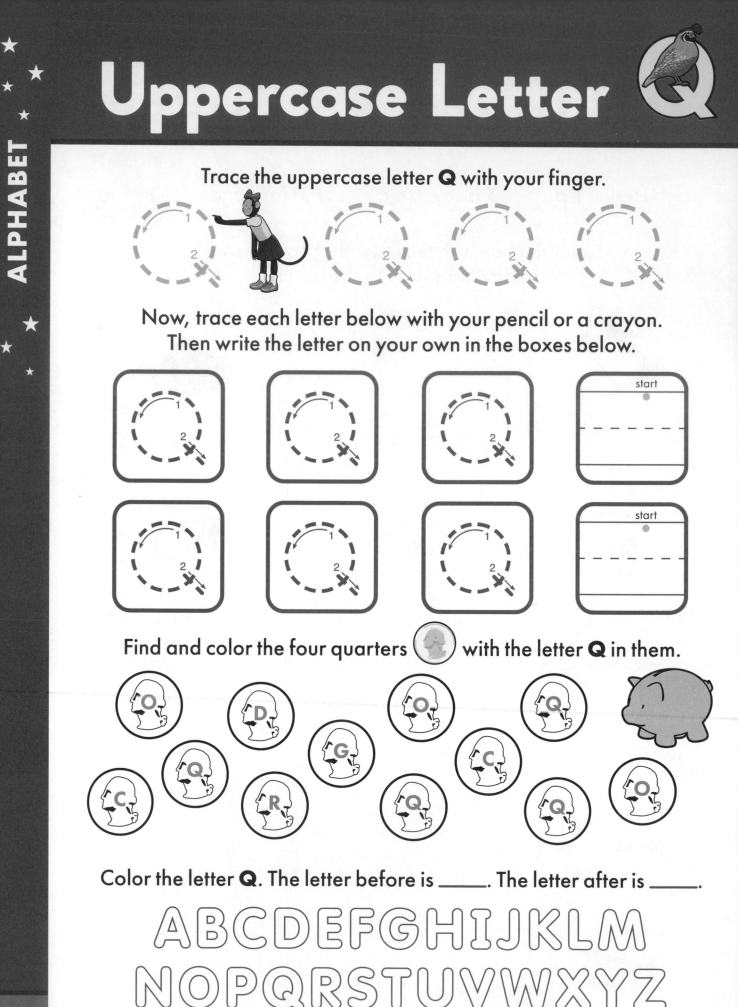

Now, trace each letter below with your pencil or a crayon.
Then write the letter on your own in the boxes below.

start

start

Find and color the four quarters with the letter **Q** in them.

Color the letter **Q**. The letter before is _____. The letter after is _____.

ABCDEFGHIJKLM
NOPQRSTUVWXYZ

Lowercase Letter q

Trace the lowercase letter **q** with your finger.

Now, trace each letter below with your pencil or a crayon.
Then write the letter on your own in the boxes below.

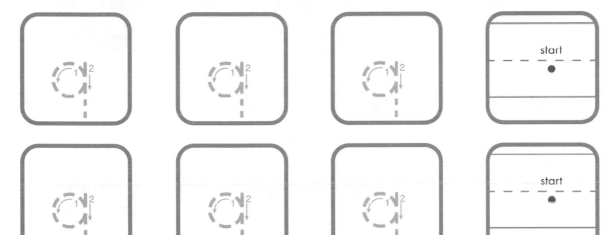

start

start

Alphabet Soup!

Find and color all lowercase **q**'s.

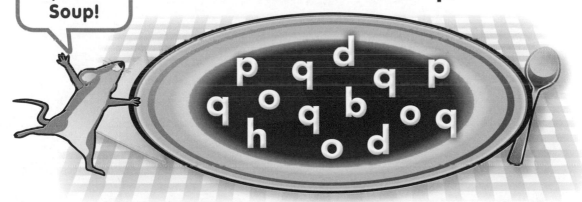

Color the letter **q**. The letter before is _____. The letter after is _____.

abcdefghijklm
nopqrstuvwxyz

Beginning Sounds

Here is **Qq**. **Qq** says **/kw/**. **Q** is for queen.

Color the box with the letter that has the same beginning sound as the picture.

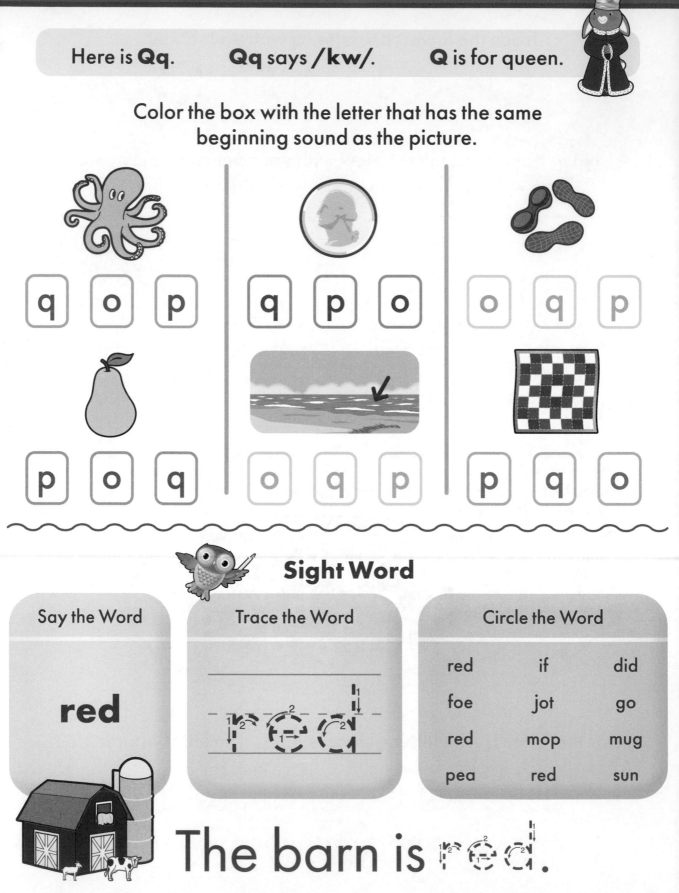

| q | o | p | | q | p | o | | o | q | p |

| p | o | q | | o | q | p | | p | q | o |

Sight Word

Say the Word	Trace the Word	Circle the Word
red		red if did foe jot go red mop mug pea red sun

The barn is red.

Uppercase Letter

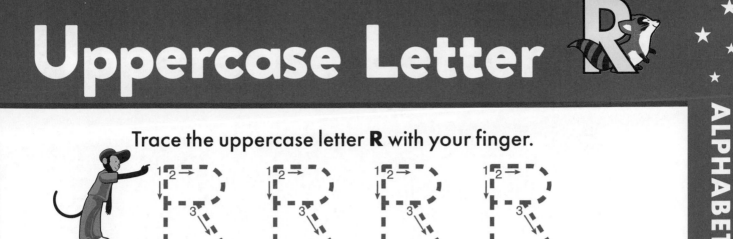

Trace the uppercase letter **R** with your finger.

Now, trace each letter below with your pencil or a crayon.
Then write the letter on your own in the boxes below.

start

start

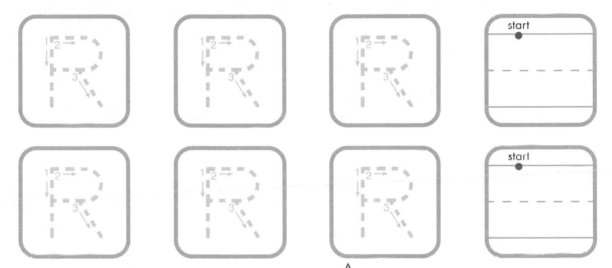

Find and color the four raindrops 💧 with the letter **R** in them.

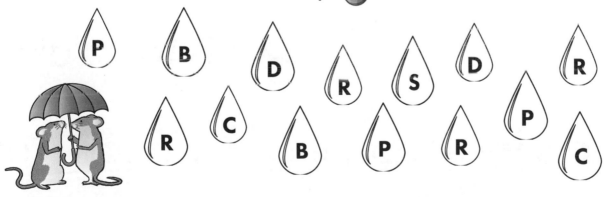

Color the letter **R**. The letter before is _____. The letter after is _____.

ABCDEFGHIJKLM
NOPQRSTUVWXYZ

Lowercase Letter r

Trace the lowercase letter **r** with your finger.

Now, trace each letter below with your pencil or a crayon.
Then write the letter on your own in the boxes below.

start

start

Trace the lowercase letter **r** to complete the word.

r is for **r**obot

r is for **r**ake

r is for **r**ooster

r is for **r**at

Color the letter **r**. The letter before is _____. The letter after is _____.

abcdefghijklm
nopqrstuvwxyz

Beginning Sounds

Here is **Rr**.   **Rr** says **/r/**.   **R** is for ring.

Color all of the pictures that begin with the **Rr** sound.

Sight Word

Say the Word	Trace the Word	Circle the Word
two		mom two art
		pen sky wet
		cup two oak
		two fee we

There are two cats.

95

Uppercase Letter S

Trace the uppercase letter **S** with your finger.

Now, trace each letter below with your pencil or a crayon.
Then write the letter on your own in the boxes below.

start

start

Find and color the four shells with the letter **S** in them.

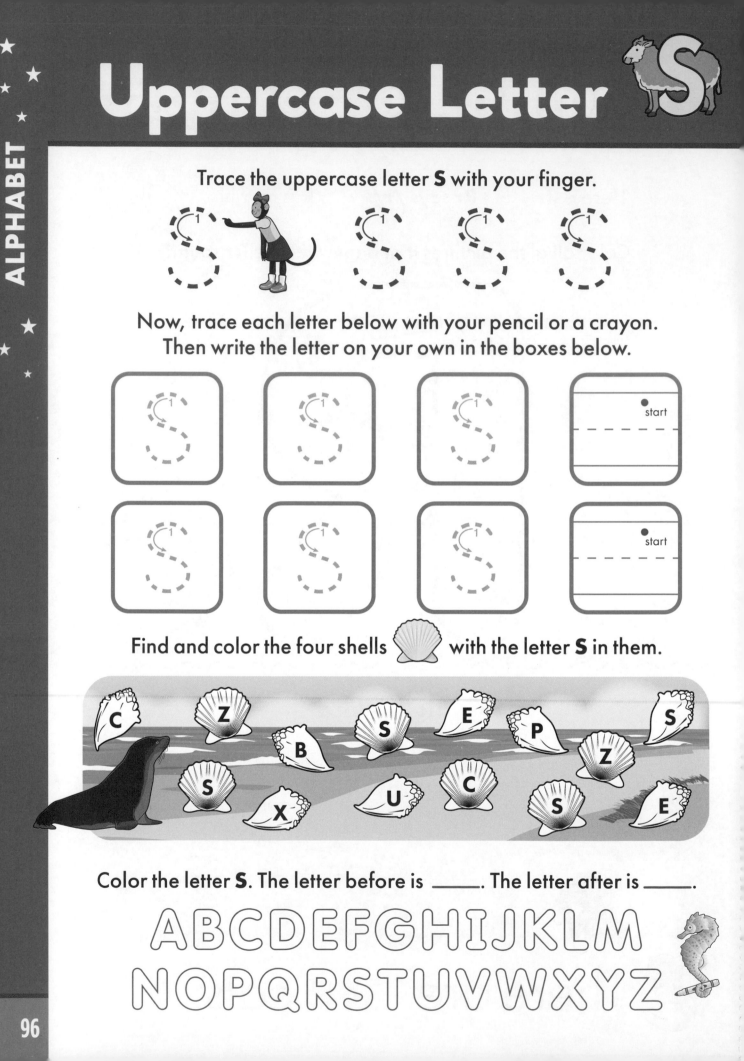

Color the letter **S**. The letter before is _____. The letter after is _____.

ABCDEFGHIJKLM
NOPQRSTUVWXYZ

Lowercase Letter s

Trace the lowercase letter **s** with your finger.

Now, trace each letter below with your pencil or a crayon.
Then write the letter on your own in the boxes below.

start

start

Find and circle all lowercase **s**'s.

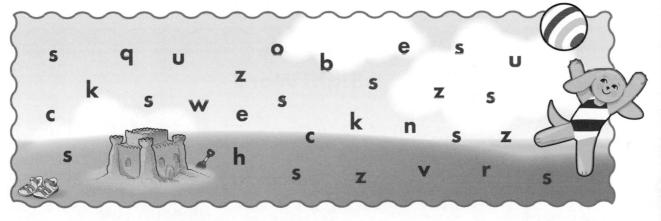

Color the letter **s**. The letter before is _____. The letter after is _____.

abcdefghijklm
nopqrstuvwxyz

97

Beginning Sounds

Here is **Ss**.   **Ss** says **/s/**.   **S** is for star.

Color the matching sock in each row.

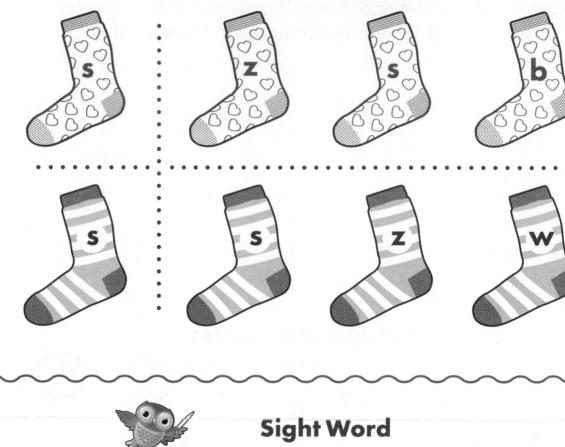

Sight Word

Say the Word	Trace the Word	Circle the Word
and	and	new sap and and bow go dog and owe ram it an

I like to play hide-and-seek.

Uppercase Letter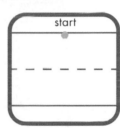

Trace the uppercase letter **T** with your finger.

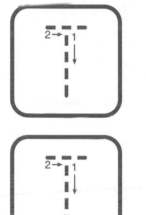

Now, trace each letter below with your pencil or a crayon.
Then write the letter on your own in the boxes below.

start

start

Find and color the four tomatoes  with the letter **T** in them.

Color the letter **T**. The letter before is _____. The letter after is _____.

ABCDEFGHIJKLM
NOPQRSTUVWXYZ

99

Lowercase Letter t

Trace the lowercase letter **t** with your finger.

Now, trace each letter below with your pencil or a crayon.
Then write the letter on your own in the boxes below.

• start

• start

Help the truck find its way to the highway
by following the path of lowercase **t**.

Color the letter **t**. The letter before is _____. The letter after is _____.

abcdefghijklm
nopqrstuvwxyz

Beginning Sounds

Here is **Tt**.   **Tt** says /**t**/.   **T** is for top.

Circle each picture that begins with the **Tt** sound.

Sight Word

Say the Word	Trace the Word	Circle the Word		
play	p l a y	play	cut	hoe
		skip	play	tree
		fan	sled	dot
		leaf	egg	play

Come play with me.

101

Uppercase Letter

Trace the uppercase letter **U** with your finger.

U U U U

Now, trace each letter below with your pencil or a crayon.
Then write the letter on your own in the boxes below.

U U U start

U U U start

Find and color the four umbrellas  with the letter **U** in them.

U O U C
V W U U

Color the letter **U**. The letter before is _____. The letter after is _____.

ABCDEFGHIJKLM
NOPQRSTUVWXYZ

Lowercase Letter u

Trace the lowercase letter **u** with your finger.

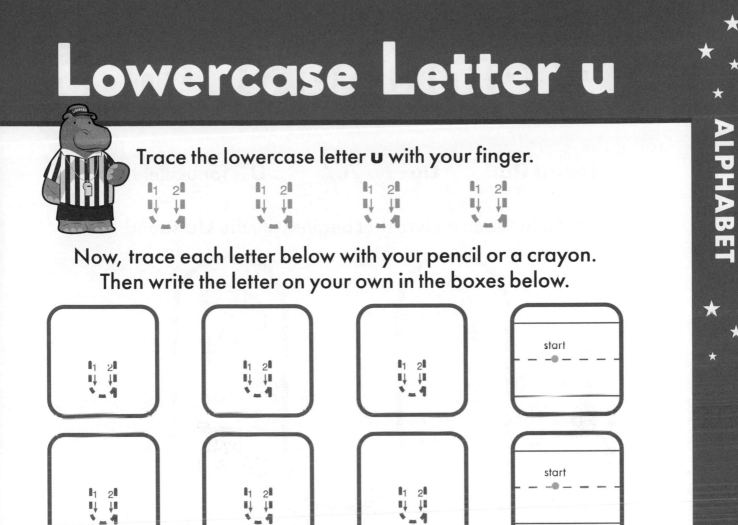

Now, trace each letter below with your pencil or a crayon.
Then write the letter on your own in the boxes below.

start

start

Color all the spaces with the letter **S green**, the letter **T blue**,
and the letter **U yellow** to reveal the hidden picture.

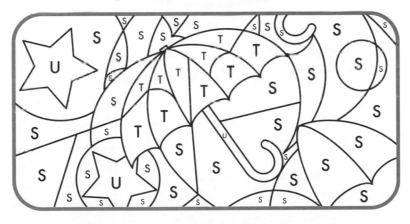

Color the letter **u**. The letter before is _____. The letter after is _____.

abcdefghijklm
nopqrstuvwxyz

Beginning Sounds

Here is **Uu**. **Uu** says **/u/**. **U** is for ukulele.

Color each picture that begins with the **Uu** sound.

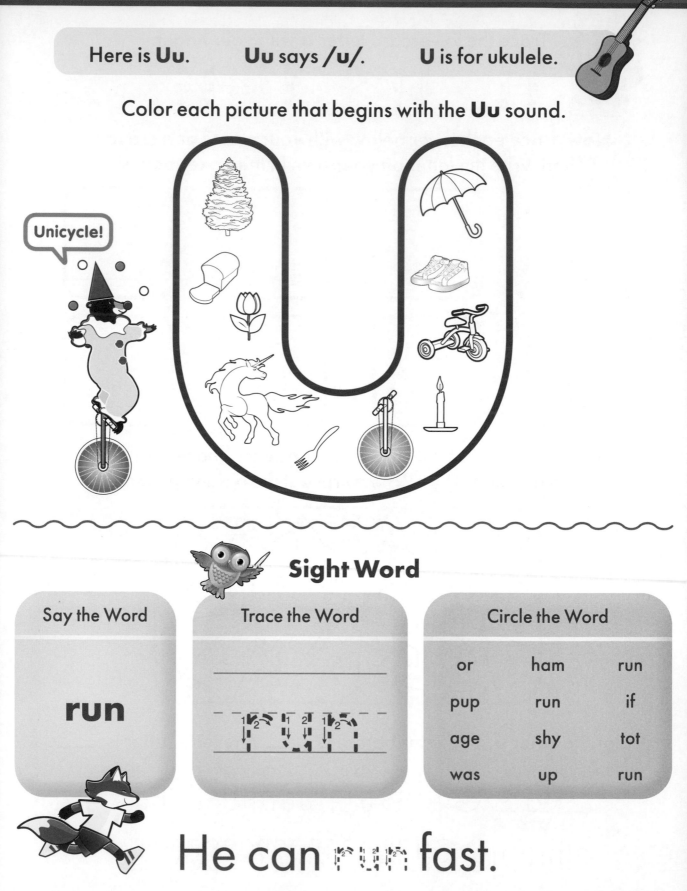

Unicycle!

Sight Word

Say the Word	Trace the Word	Circle the Word
run	_____	or ham run
	r̶u̶n̶	pup run if
		age shy tot
		was up run

He can run fast.

Uppercase Letter

Trace the uppercase letter **V** with your finger.

Now, trace each letter below with your pencil or a crayon.
Then write the letter on your own in the boxes below.

start

start

Find and circle the four vegetables with the letter **V** in them.

Color the letter **V**. The letter before is _____. The letter after is _____.

ABCDEFGHIJKLM
NOPQRSTUVWXYZ

Lowercase Letter v

Trace the lowercase letter **v** with your finger.

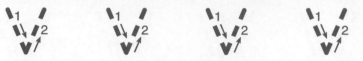

Now, trace each letter below with your pencil or a crayon.
Then write the letter on your own in the boxes below.

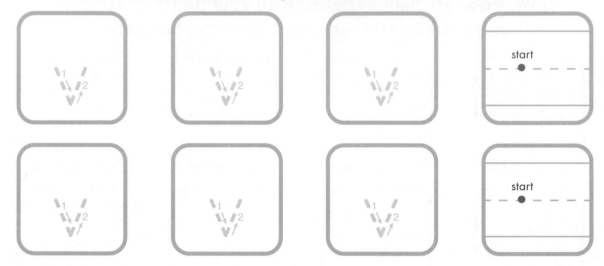

start

start

Help the batter get to the game by following the path of lowercase **v**.

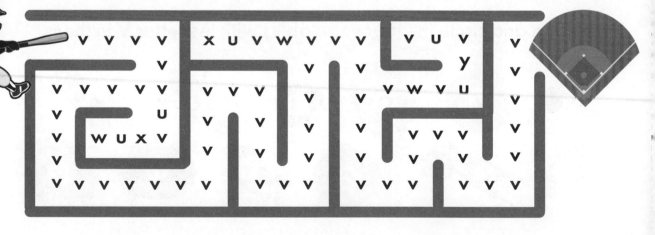

Color the letter **v**. The letter before is _____. The letter after is _____.

abcdefghijklm
nopqrstuvwxyz

Beginning Sounds

Here is **Vv**.   **Vv** says **/v/**.   **V** is for violets.

Color the box with the letter that has the same beginning sound as the picture.

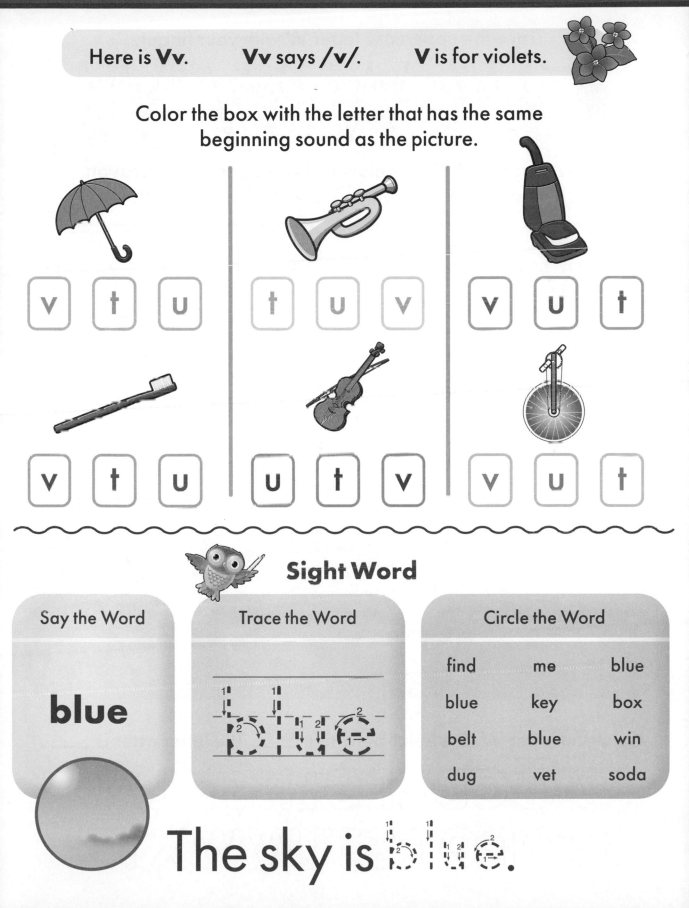

v	t	u
t	u	v
v	u	t

v	t	u
u	t	v
v	u	t

Sight Word

Say the Word

blue

Trace the Word

Circle the Word

find	me	blue
blue	key	box
belt	blue	win
dug	vet	soda

The sky is blue.

Uppercase Letter

Trace the uppercase letter **W** with your finger.

Now, trace each letter below with your pencil or a crayon.
Then write the letter on your own in the boxes below.

start

start

Find and color the four whales  with the letter **W** in them.

Color the letter **W**. The letter before is _____. The letter after is _____.

ABCDEFGHIJKLM
NOPQRSTUVWXYZ

Lowercase Letter w

Trace the lowercase letter **w** with your finger.

Now, trace each letter below with your pencil or a crayon.
Then write the letter on your own in the boxes below.

start

start

Trace the lowercase letter **w** to complete the word.

w is for **w**atch

w is for **w**agon

w is for **w**alrus

w is for **w**olf

Color the letter **w**. The letter before is _____. The letter after is _____.

abcdefghijklm
nopqrstuvwxyz

Beginning Sounds

Here is **Ww**.   **Ww** says **/w/**.   **W** is for wig.

Color all of the pictures that begin with the **Ww** sound.

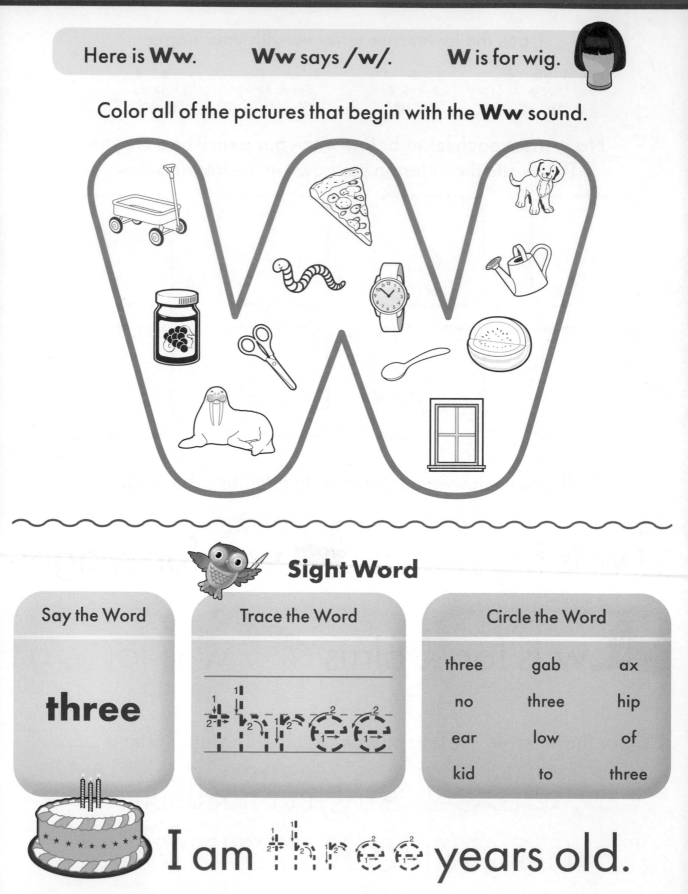

Sight Word

Say the Word	Trace the Word	Circle the Word
three		

three	gab	ax
no	three	hip
ear	low	of
kid	to	three

I am three years old.

Uppercase Letter X

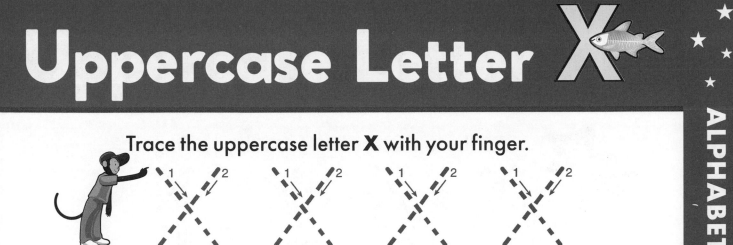

Trace the uppercase letter **X** with your finger.

Now, trace each letter below with your pencil or a crayon.
Then write the letter on your own in the boxes below.

start

start

Find and color the four X-rays with the letter **X** in them.

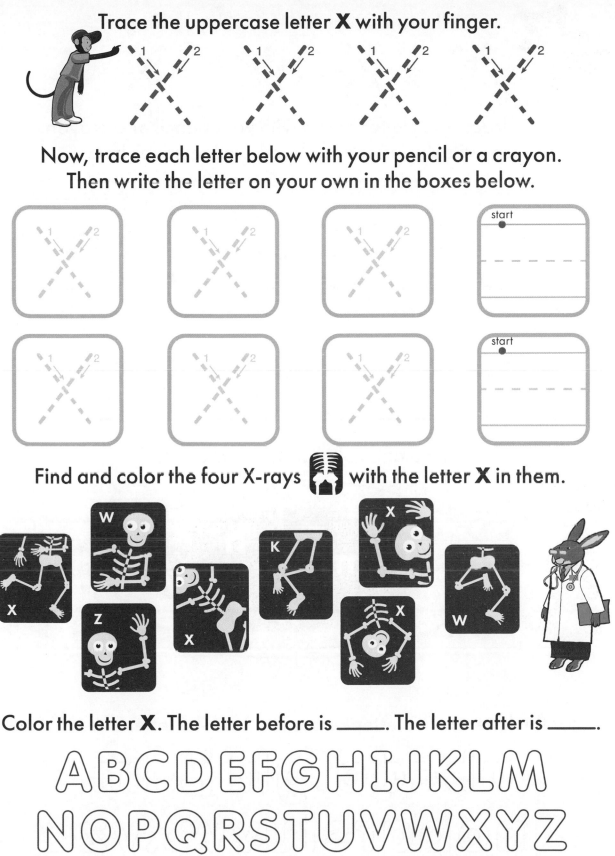

Color the letter **X**. The letter before is _____. The letter after is _____.

ABCDEFGHIJKLM
NOPQRSTUVWXYZ

ALPHABET

111

Lowercase Letter x

Trace the lowercase letter **x** with your finger.

Now, trace each letter below with your pencil or a crayon.
Then write the letter on your own in the boxes below.

start

start

Find and color all lowercase **x**'s.

Alphabet Soup!

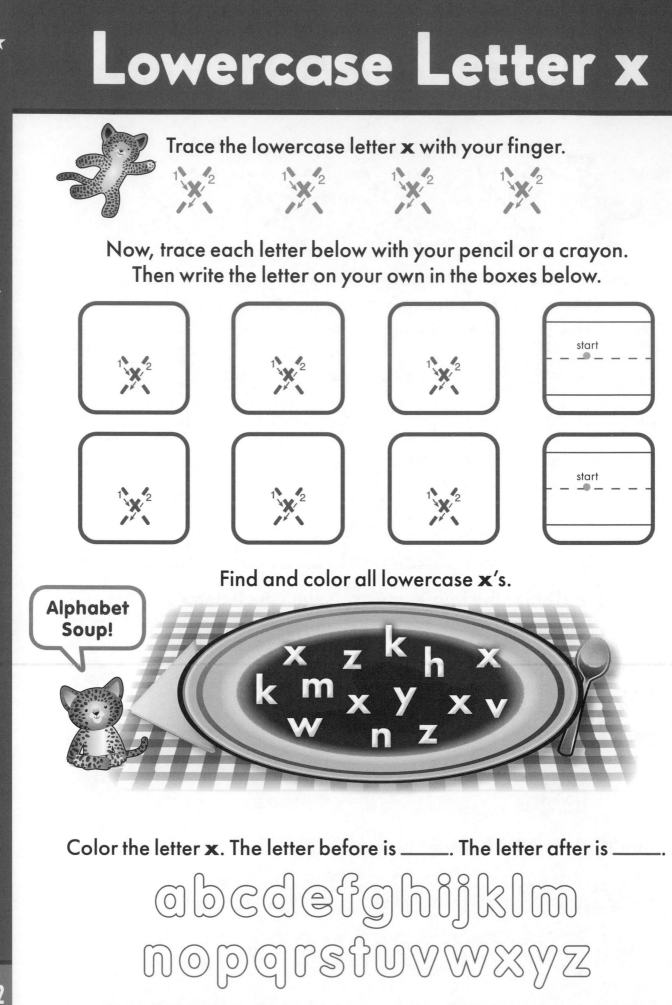

Color the letter **x**. The letter before is _____. The letter after is _____.

abcdefghijklm
nopqrstuvwxyz

Beginning Sounds

Here is **Xx**.   **Xx** says **/x/**.   **X** is for xylophone.

Not many words begin with the **Xx** sound.
Can you circle the words that end with the **Xx** sound?

mix! fix!

Sight Word

Say the Word	Trace the Word	Circle the Word
in		

on	is	if
in	an	on
no	in	is
it	it	in

He is in the car.

Uppercase Letter Y

Trace the uppercase letter **Y** with your finger.

Now, trace each letter below with your pencil or a crayon.
Then write the letter on your own in the boxes below.

start

start

Find and color the four balls of yarn with the letter **Y** in them.

V N V W
Y X Y
W H V
Z Y K

Color the letter **Y**. The letter before is _____. The letter after is _____.

ABCDEFGHIJKLM
NOPQRSTUVWXYZ

Lowercase Letter y

Trace the lowercase letter **y** with your finger.

Now, trace each letter below with your pencil or a crayon.
Then write the letter on your own in the boxes below.

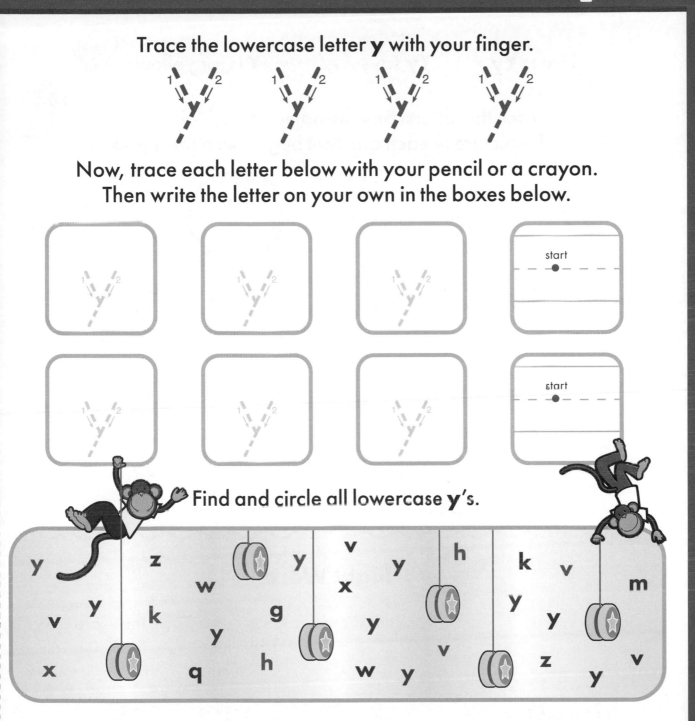

start

start

Find and circle all lowercase **y**'s.

y	z		y	v	h	k v
	w			x		m
v	y	k	g		y	y
		y		y		
x	q	h	w	y	v	z v
						y

Color the letter **y**. The letter before is _____. The letter after is _____.

abcdefghijklm
nopqrstuvwxyz

115

Beginning Sounds

Here is **Yy**.   **Yy** says **/y/**.   **Y** is for yellow.

Trace the letters. Say the name of each picture.
Color the picture in each box that begins with the **Yy** sound.

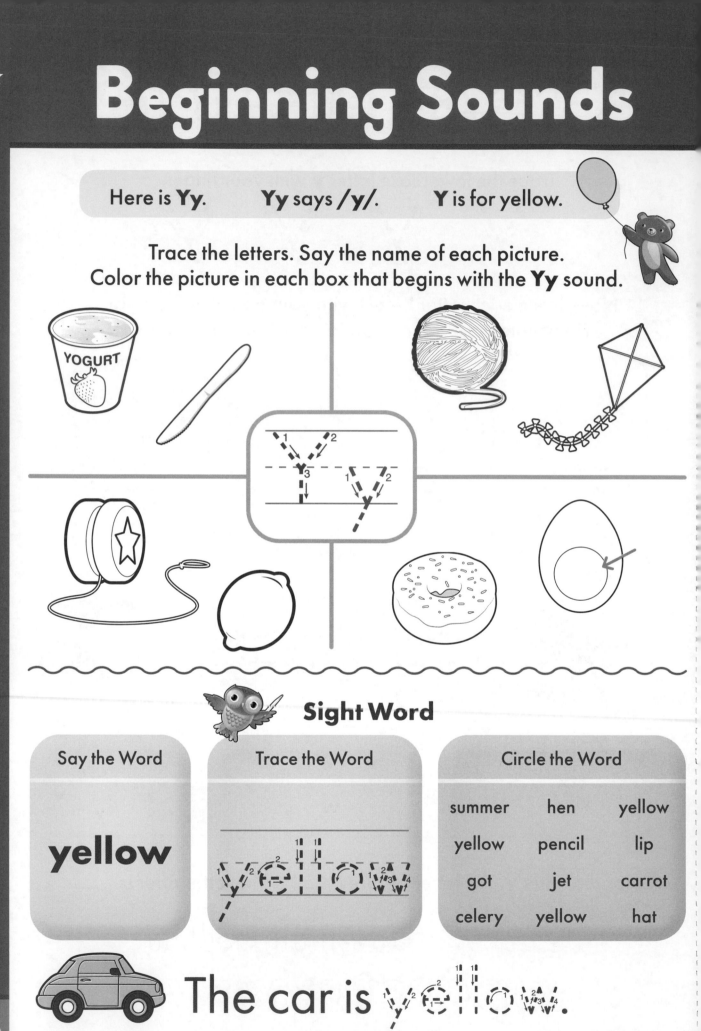

Sight Word

Say the Word	Trace the Word	Circle the Word
yellow		summer hen yellow yellow pencil lip got jet carrot celery yellow hat

The car is yellow.

Uppercase Letter

Trace the uppercase letter **Z** with your finger.

Now, trace each letter below with your pencil or a crayon.
Then write the letter on your own in the boxes below.

start

start

Find and color the four zebras with the letter **Z** in them.

Color the letter **Z**. The letter before is _____.

A B C D E F G H I J K L M
N O P Q R S T U V W X Y Z

117

Lowercase Letter z

Trace the lowercase letter **z** with your finger.

Now, trace each letter below with your pencil or a crayon.
Then write the letter on your own in the boxes below.

start

start

Help the zebra get through the zoo by following the path of lowercase **z**.

EXIT

Color the letter **z**. The letter before is _____.

abcdefghijklm
nopqrstuvwxyz

Beginning Sounds

Here is **Zz**.   **Zz** says **/z/**.   **Z** is for zebra.

Color the box with the letter that has the same beginning sound of the picture.

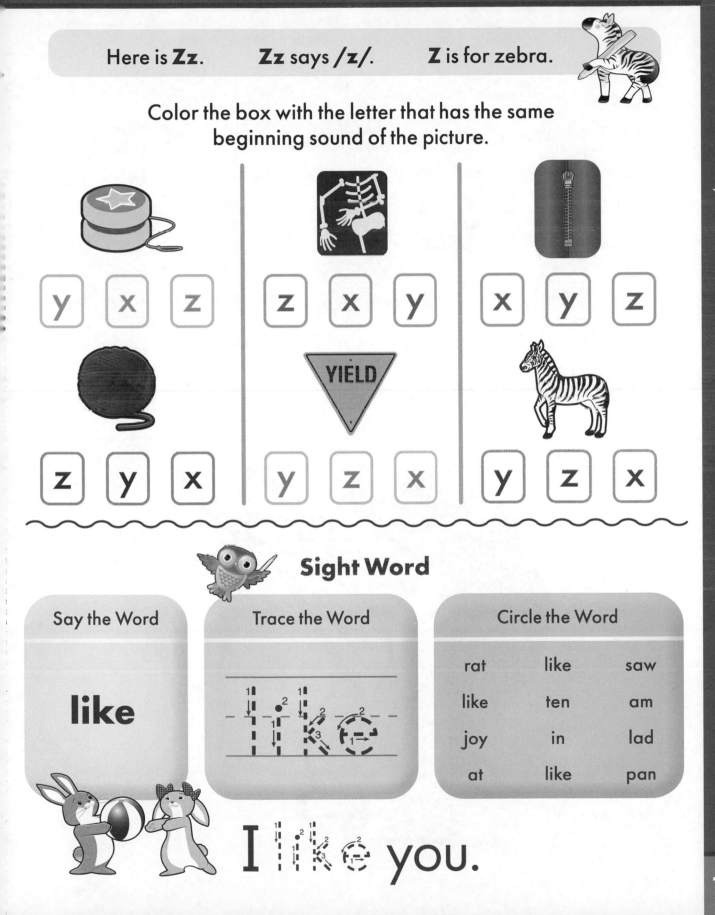

| y | x | z | | z | x | y | | x | y | z |

| z | y | x | | y | z | x | | y | z | x |

Sight Word

Say the Word	Trace the Word	Circle the Word
like		rat like saw
		like ten am
		joy in lad
		at like pan

I like you.

NUMBERS & COUNTING

ZERO

Trace the number **0** on the first line with your finger.
Then write the number **0** by following the arrows on the next two lines.

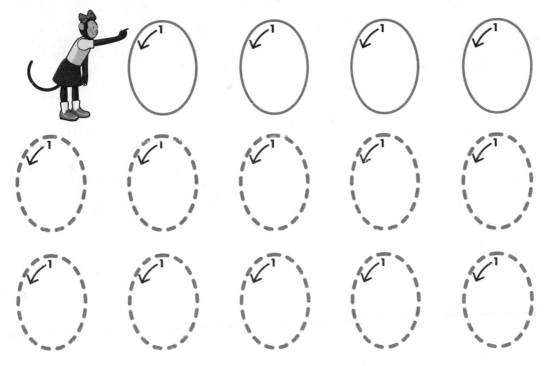

Count the dots in the ten-frame and then circle the
die or dice that add up to the same number of dots.

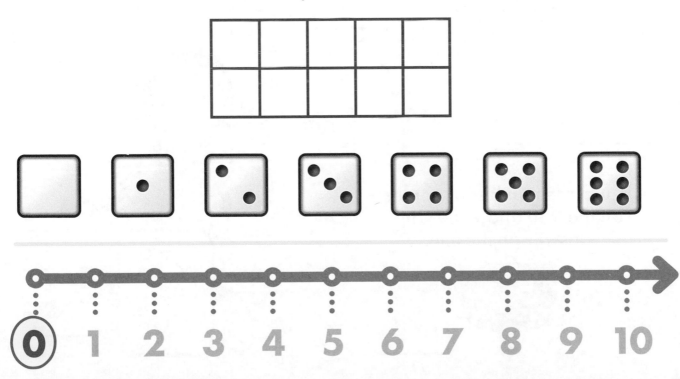

0 1 2 3 4 5 6 7 8 9 10

0 ZERO

Practice writing the number **0** by following the arrows.

Circle all the number **0**s.

9   0   0   8   3

6   3   3   0

0   6   9   2

How many **0**s did you find?

Color the dog with **0** spots.

Making 0
Write the numbers that add up to **0**.

_____ + _____ =

Count the number of apples on the tree and write your answer on the line.

_____

What number comes **after 0**?

_____

Trace the number **1** on the first line with your finger.
Then write the number **1** by following the arrows on the next two lines.

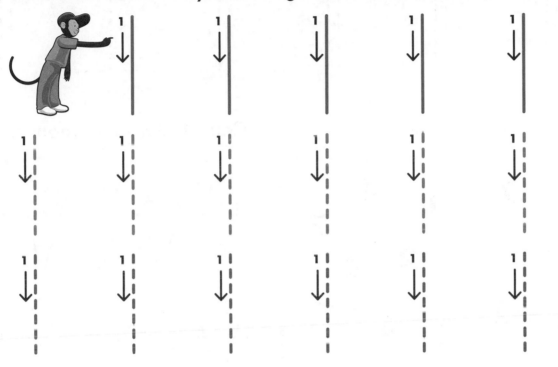

Count the dots in the ten-frame and then circle the
die or dice that add up to the same number of dots.

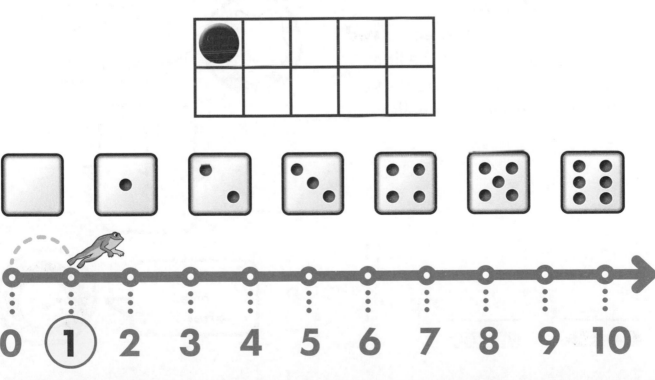

0 1 2 3 4 5 6 7 8 9 10

1

ONE

Practice writing the number **1** by following the arrows.

Circle all the number **1**s.

1 7 1 4
7
5 1 2
4
1 2
1 3

How many **1**s did you find?

Color **1** of the ice cream cones.

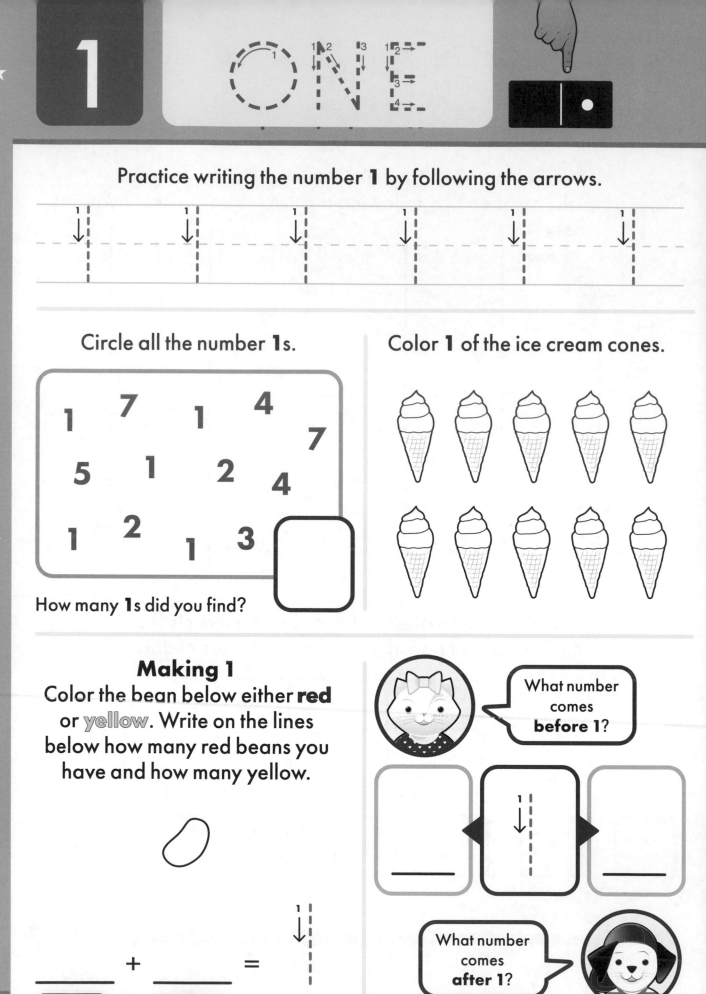

Making 1
Color the bean below either **red** or yellow. Write on the lines below how many red beans you have and how many yellow.

What number comes **before 1**?

What number comes **after 1**?

_____ + _____ = 1

2

Trace the number **2** on the first line with your finger.
Then write the number **2** by following the arrows on the next two lines.

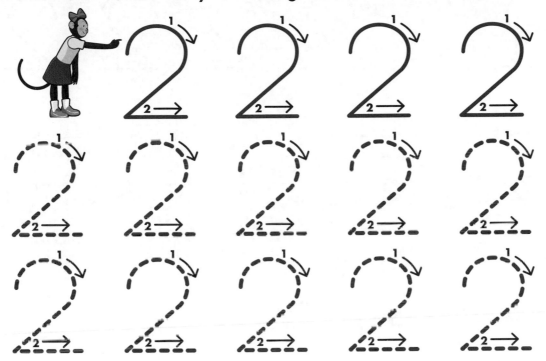

Count the dots in the ten-frame and then circle the
die or dice that add up to the same number of dots.

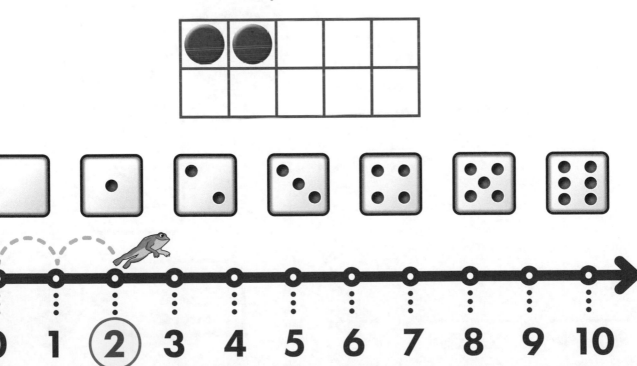

0   1   (2)   3   4   5   6   7   8   9   10

2

TWO

Practice writing the number **2** by following the arrows.

2 2 2 2 2 2

Circle all the number **2**s.

3 2 4 2 7
6 2 2 2
2 5 2 5

How many **2**s did you find?

Color **2** of the owls.

Making 2
Color the beans below either **red** or yellow. Write on the lines below how many red beans you have and how many yellow.

_____ + _____ = 2

What number comes **before 2**?

_____ 2 _____

What number comes **after 2**?

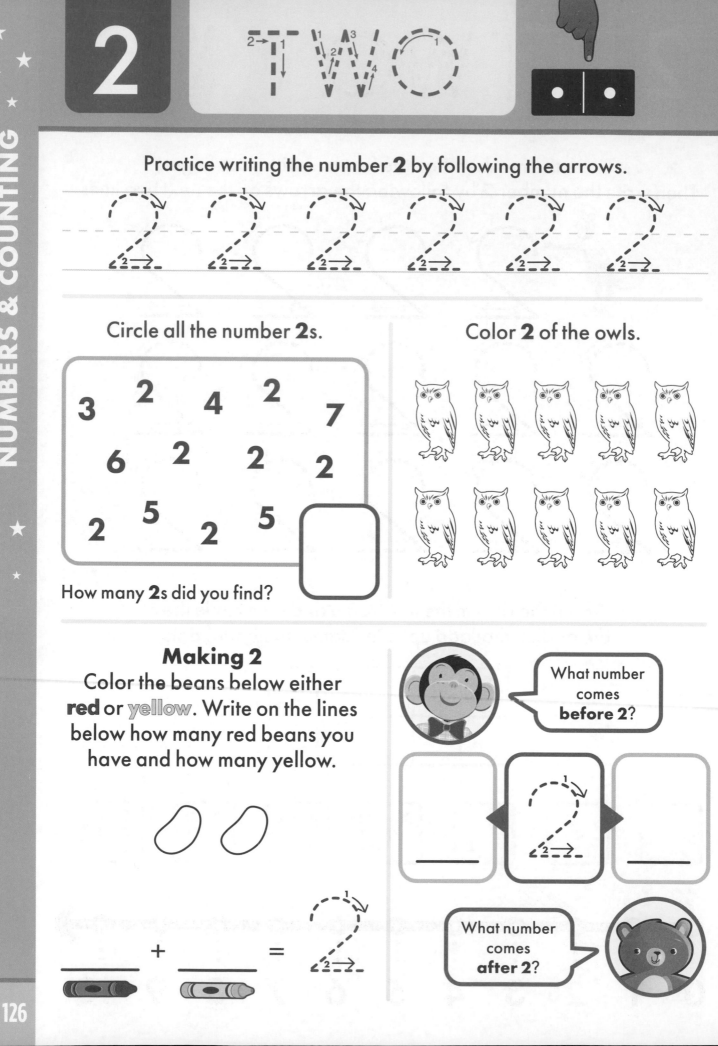

3

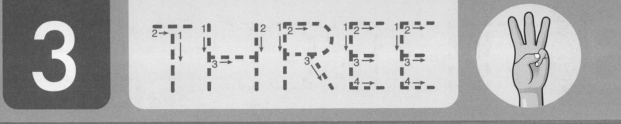

Trace the number **3** on the first line with your finger.
Then write the number **3** by following the arrows on the next two lines.

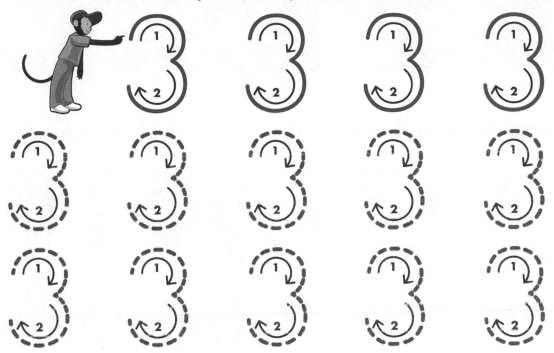

Count the dots in the ten-frame and then circle the
die or dice that add up to the same number of dots.

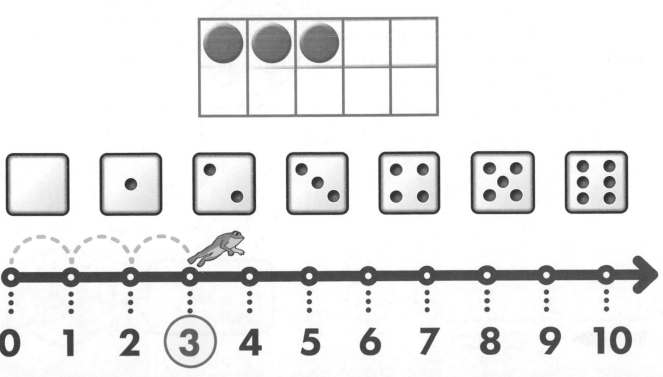

0   1   2   (3)   4   5   6   7   8   9   10

3

THREE

Practice writing the number **3** by following the arrows.

3 3 3 3 3 3

Circle all the number **3**s.

5 3   6   3
              2
9   3   5   3

3   0   3
        2

How many **3**s did you find?

Color **3** of the robots.

Making 3
Color the beans below either **red** or yellow. Write on the lines below how many red beans you have and how many yellow.

What number comes **before** 3?

3

_____ + _____ = 3

What number comes **after** 3?

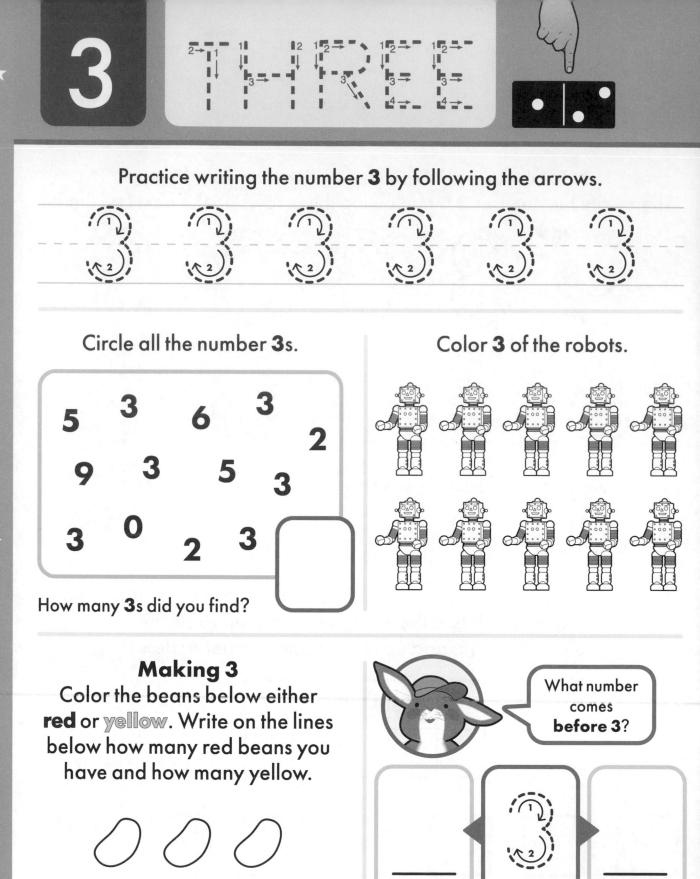

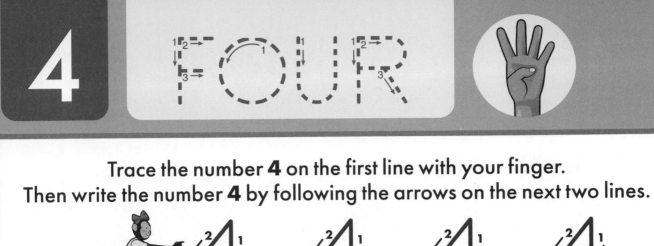

4

Trace the number **4** on the first line with your finger.
Then write the number **4** by following the arrows on the next two lines.

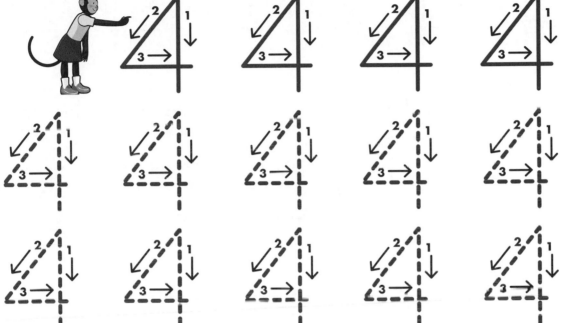

Count the dots in the ten-frame and then circle the
die or dice that add up to the same number of dots.

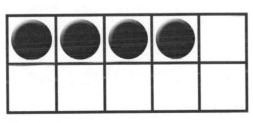

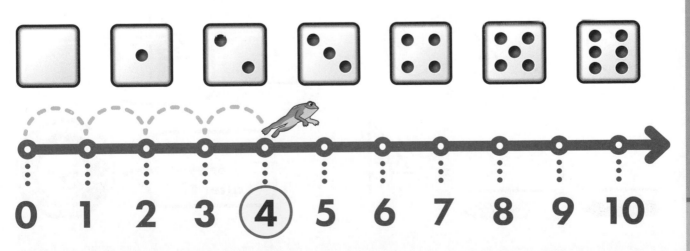

0   1   2   3   (4)   5   6   7   8   9   10

4

FOUR

Practice writing the number **4** by following the arrows.

Circle all the number **4**s.

4 7 4 4
4
2 4 4 3
4 5 4 7

How many **4**s did you find?

Color **4** of the leaves.

Making 4
Color the beans below either **red** or yellow. Write on the lines below how many red beans you have and how many yellow.

___ + ___ = 4

What number comes **before 4**?

What number comes **after 4**?

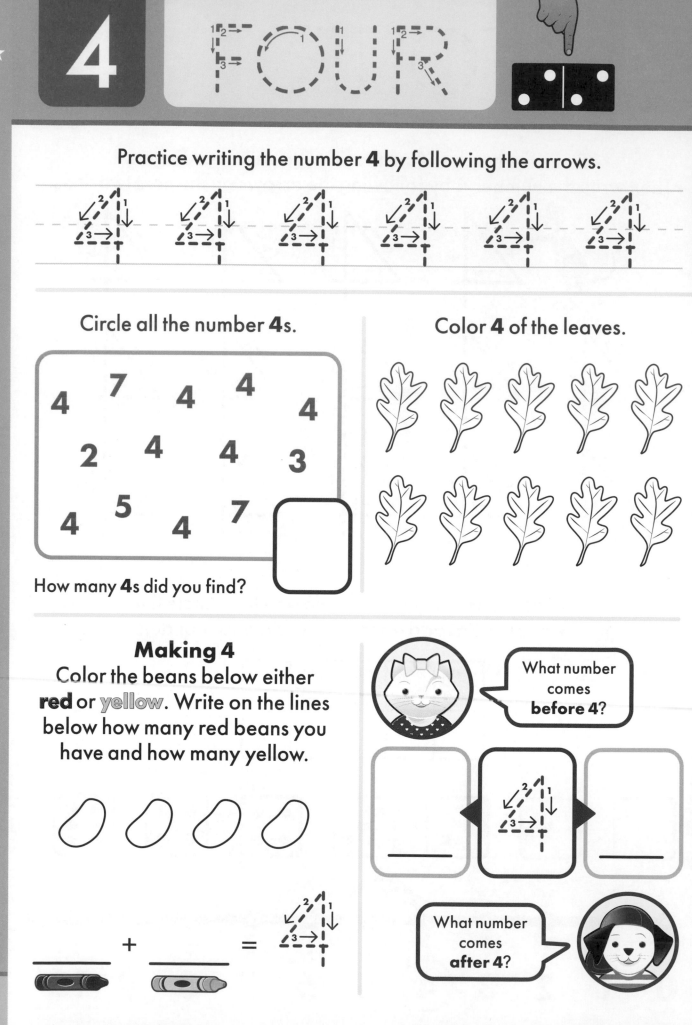

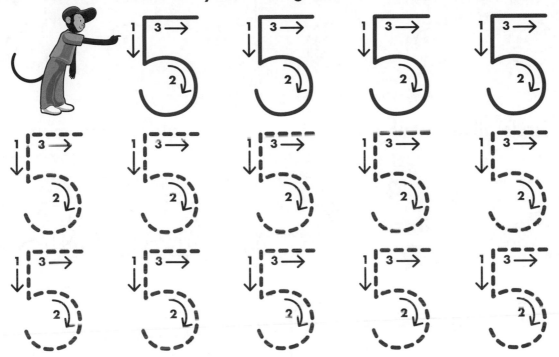

Trace the number **5** on the first line with your finger.
Then write the number **5** by following the arrows on the next two lines.

Count the dots in the ten-frame and then circle the
die or dice that add up to the same number of dots.

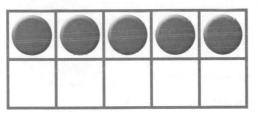

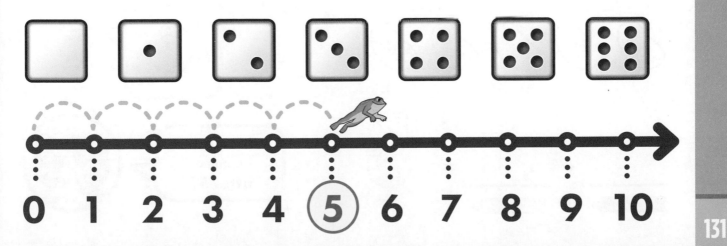

0 1 2 3 4 (5) 6 7 8 9 10

5

Practice writing the number **5** by following the arrows.

Circle all the number **5**s.

5   7   3   4
          5
  2   5   9
          7
3   7   5
      4

How many **5**s did you find?

Color **5** of the cats.

Making 5
Color the beans below either **red** or yellow. Write on the lines below how many red beans you have and how many yellow.

____ + ____ = 5

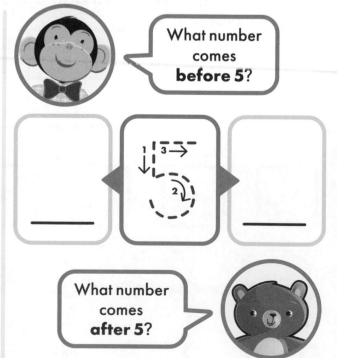

What number comes **before 5**?

____   5   ____

What number comes **after 5**?

Numbers 1-5

Draw a line from each number below to the cake
with that number of birthday candles.

3 1 5 2 4

Color all

1s green 2s yellow 3s blue
4s red 5s brown

4 1 3 5 2
5 4 2 4 3
2 4 1 5 3 5

Numbers 1–5

Count the number of each kind of zoo animal and write the number in the box.

Color the number of vegetables indicated by the number on the left.

Numbers 1–5

Cut on the dotted lines below to make your own flashcards.
Then use the cards to practice counting from 1 to 5.

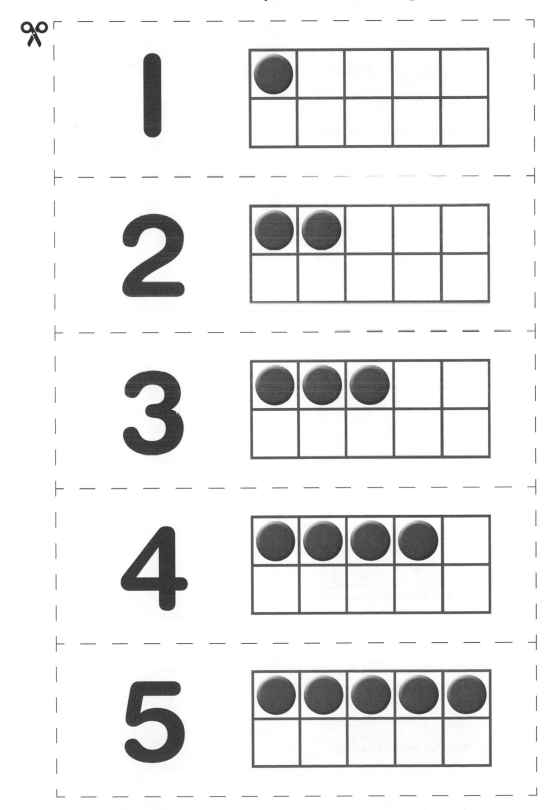

Numbers 1–5

Cut on the dotted lines below to make your own flashcards.
Then use the cards to practice counting from 1 to 5.

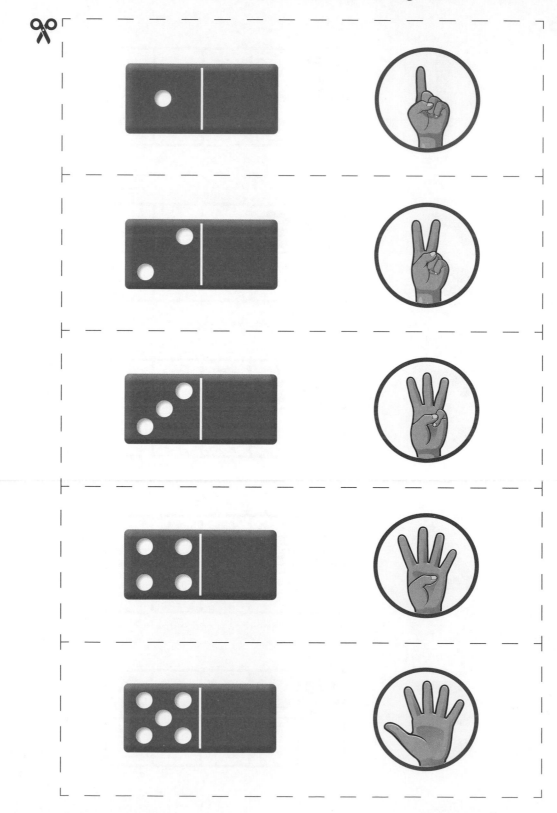

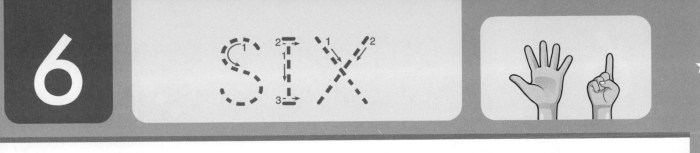

Trace the number **6** on the first line with your finger.
Then write the number **6** by following the arrows on the next two lines.

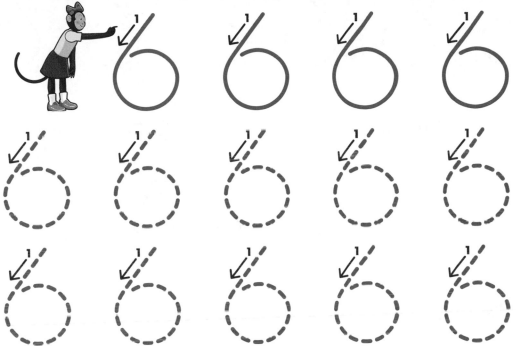

Count the dots in the ten-frame and then circle the
die or dice that add up to the same number of dots.

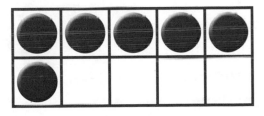

0 1 2 3 4 5 (6) 7 8 9 10

6 SIX

Practice writing the number **6** by following the arrows.

Circle all the number **6**s.

9   6   6   8
          6
5   8   6   9
   6   6   6
6   3

How many **6**s did you find?

Color **6** of the hats.

Making 6
Color the beans below either **red** or yellow. Write on the lines below how many red beans you have and how many yellow.

___ + ___ =

What number comes **before 6**?

What number comes **after 6**?

Trace the number **7** on the first line with your finger.
Then write the number **7** by following the arrows on the next two lines.

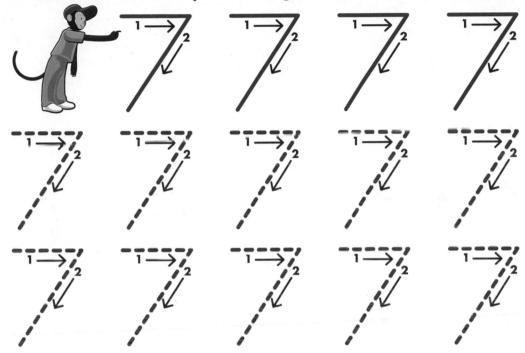

Count the dots in the ten-frame and then circle the
die or dice that add up to the same number of dots.

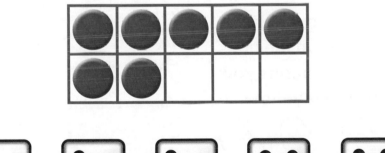

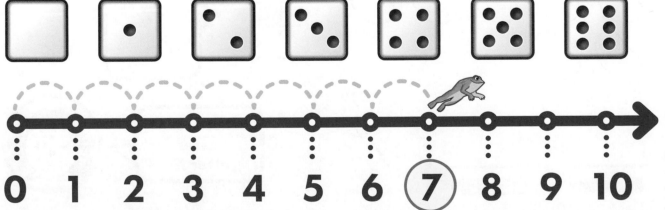

0 1 2 3 4 5 6 (7) 8 9 10

7 SEVEN

Practice writing the number **7** by following the arrows.

Circle all the number **7**s.

7 7   4   5
7   7
1   5   7   1
7   2   7   3

How many **7**s did you find?

Color **7** of the penguins.

Making 7
Color the beans below either **red** or yellow. Write on the lines below how many red beans you have and how many yellow.

___ + ___ = 7

What number comes **before 7**?

7

What number comes **after 7**?

8

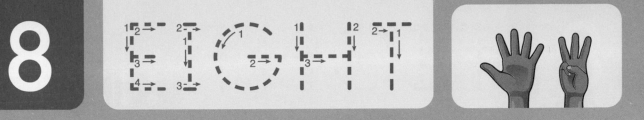

Trace the number **8** on the first line with your finger.
Then write the number **8** by following the arrows on the next two lines.

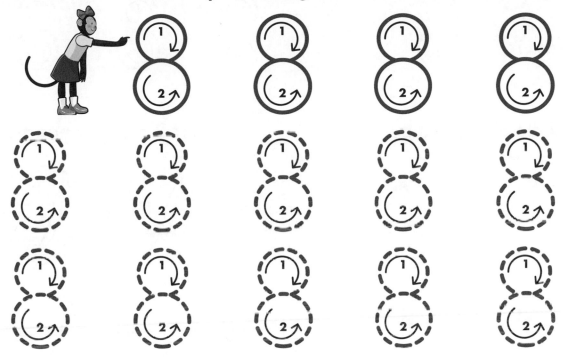

Count the dots in the ten-frame and then circle the
die or dice that add up to the same number of dots.

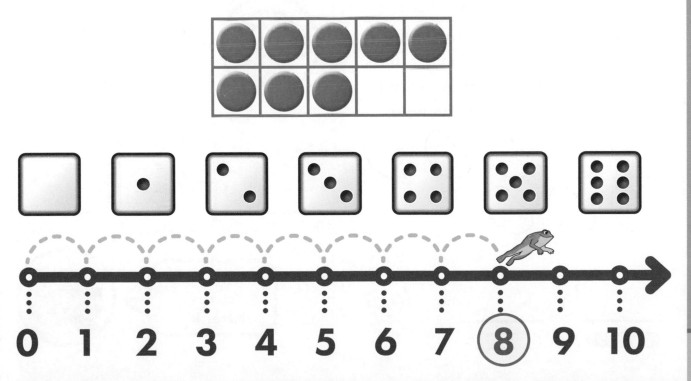

0 1 2 3 4 5 6 7 (8) 9 10

8

EIGHT

Practice writing the number **8** by following the arrows.

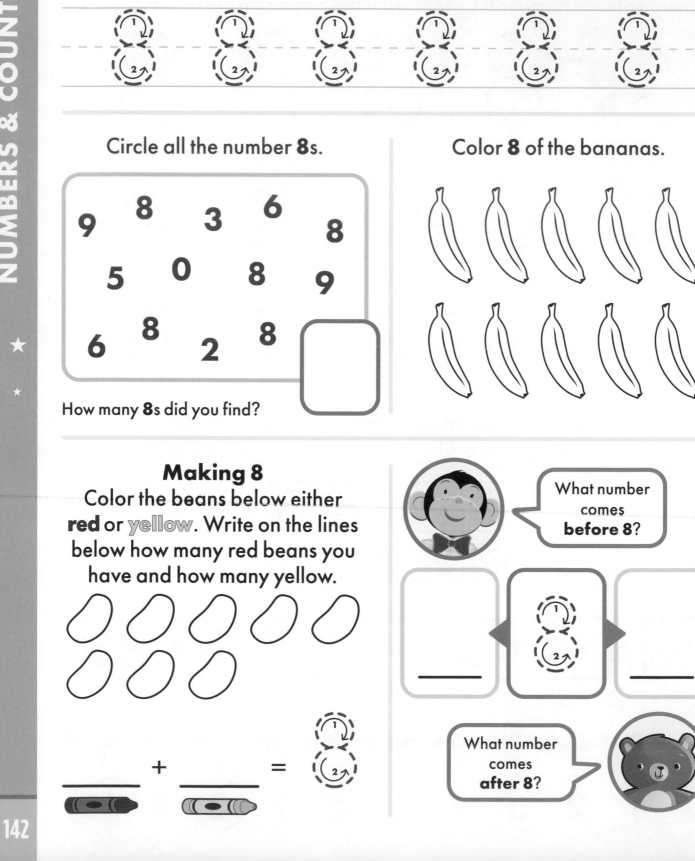

Circle all the number **8**s.

9 8 3 6
        8
5 0 8 9
6 8 2 8

How many **8**s did you find?

Color **8** of the bananas.

Making 8
Color the beans below either **red** or yellow. Write on the lines below how many red beans you have and how many yellow.

___ + ___ =

What number comes **before 8**?

What number comes **after 8**?

9

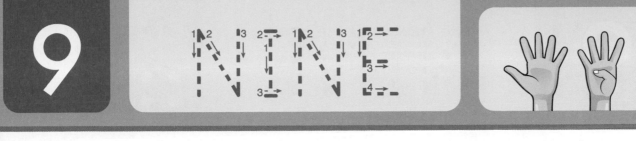

Trace the number **9** on the first line with your finger.
Then write the number **9** by following the arrows on the next two lines.

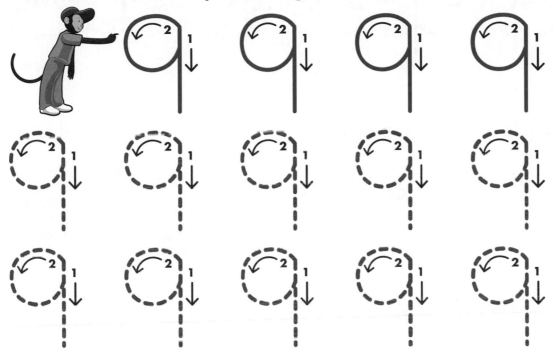

Count the dots in the ten-frame and then circle the
die or dice that add up to the same number of dots.

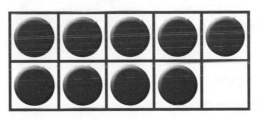

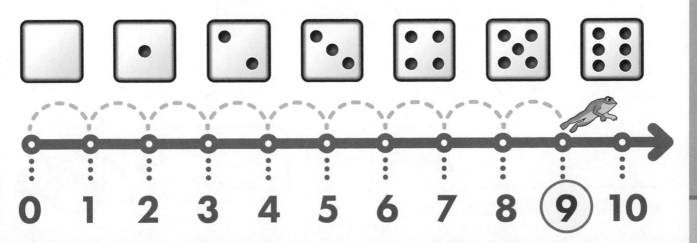

0 1 2 3 4 5 6 7 8 (9) 10

143

9

NINE

Practice writing the number **9** by following the arrows.

9 9 9 9 9 9

Circle all the number **9**s.

6 8 0 6
9
6 8 9 3
5 2 9 6

How many **9**s did you find?

Color **9** of the seahorses.

Making 9
Color the beans below either **red** or yellow. Write on the lines below how many red beans you have and how many yellow.

____ + ____ =

What number comes **before 9**?

What number comes **after 9**?

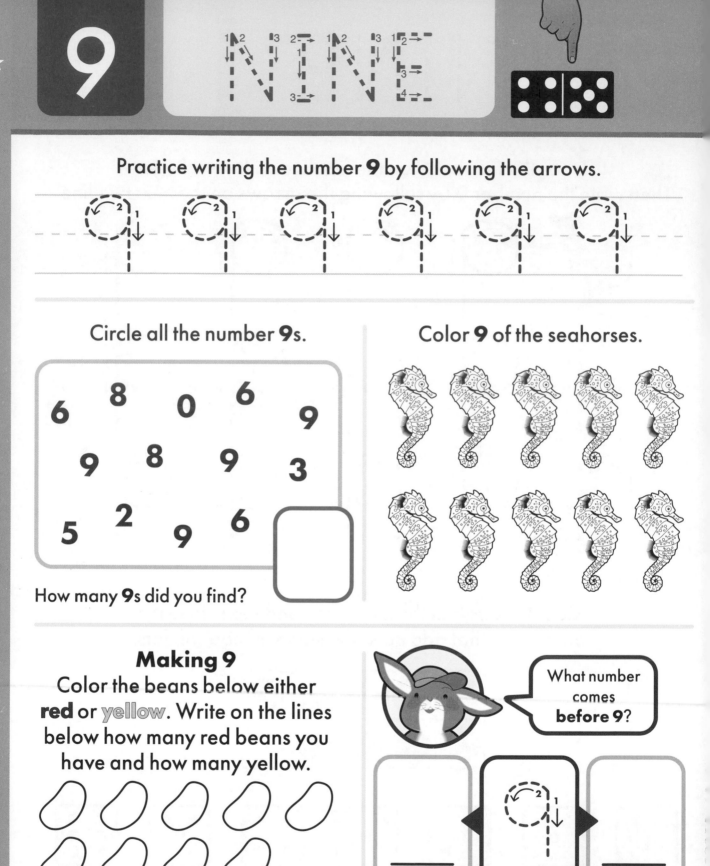

Trace the number **10** on the first line with your finger.
Then write the number **10** by following the arrows on the next two lines.

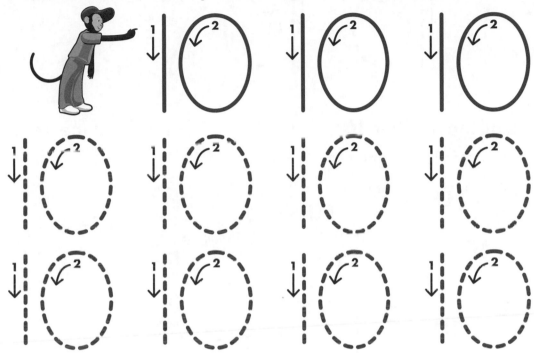

Count the dots in the ten-frame and then circle the
die or dice that add up to the same number of dots.

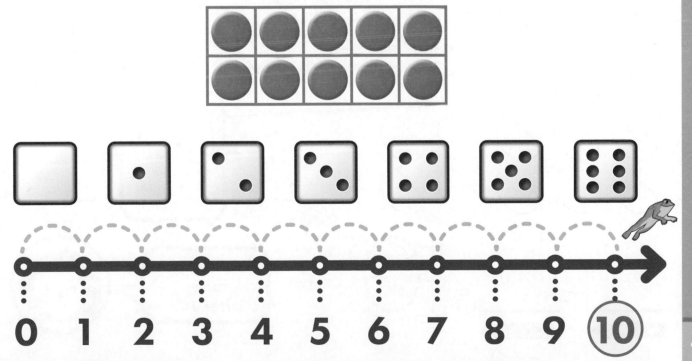

0 1 2 3 4 5 6 7 8 9 (10)

10

TEN

Practice writing the number **10** by following the arrows.

Circle all the number **10**s.

11 0 9
10 10
6 10 1 12
4 7
11 10

How many **10**s did you find?

Color **10** of the trees.

Making 10

Color the beans below either **red** or yellow. Write on the lines below how many red beans you have and how many yellow.

+ = 10

What number comes **before 10**?

What number comes **after 10**?

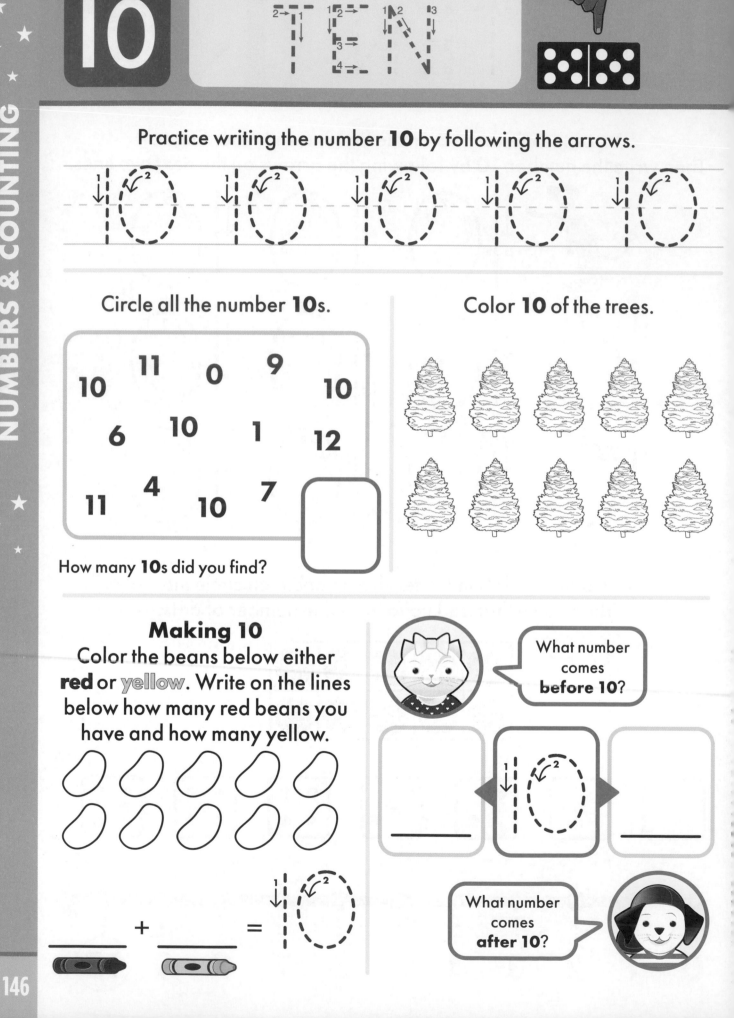

Numbers 1–10

Color the number of birds shown in each circle.

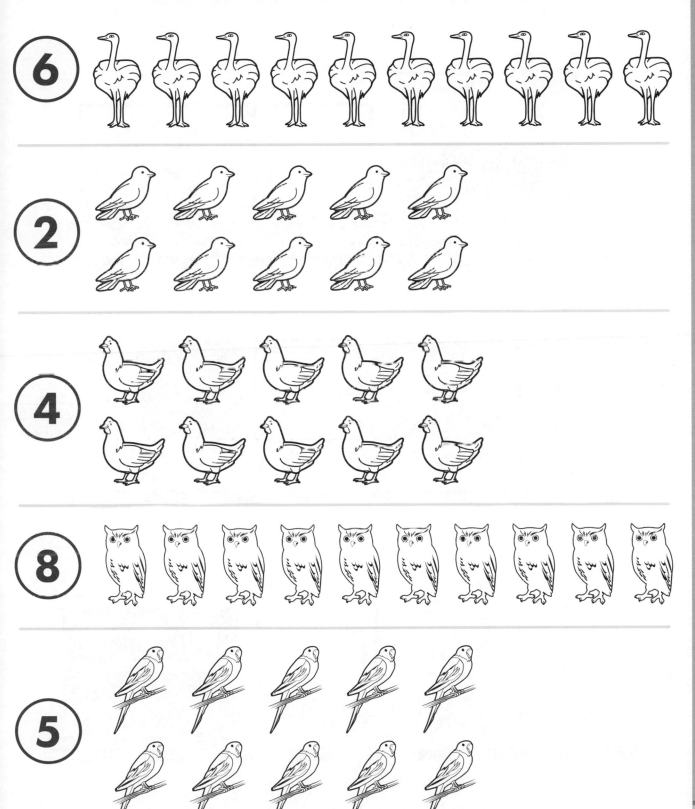

6

2

4

8

5

Numbers 1–10

Trace each number. Fill in the missing numbers.

Numbers 1–10

Cut on the dotted lines below to make your own flashcards.
Then use the cards to practice counting from 6 to 10.

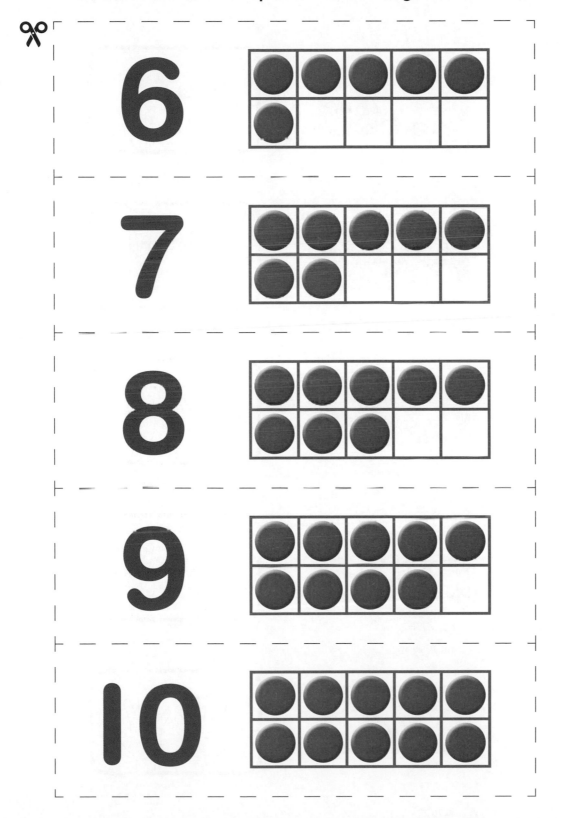

Numbers 1–10

Cut on the dotted lines below to make your own flashcards.
Then use the cards to practice counting from 6 to 10.

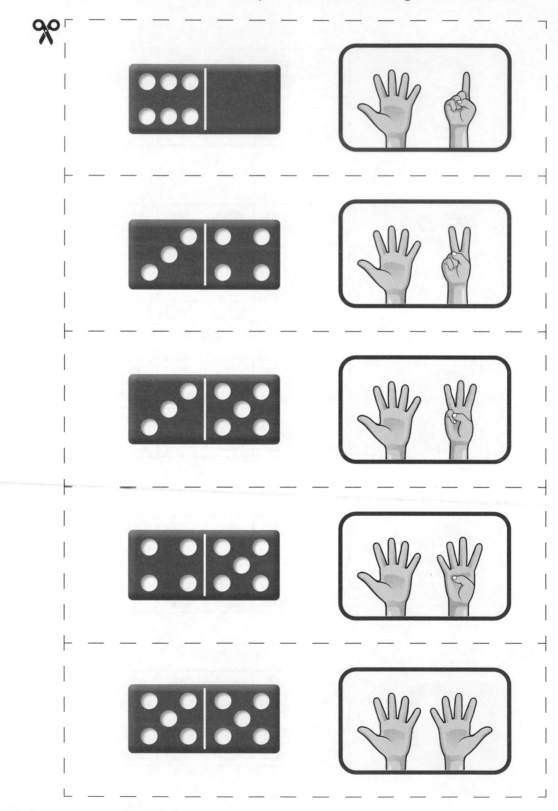

11

ELEVEN

Trace the number **11** on the first line with your finger.
Then write the number **11** by following the arrows on the second line.

Count how many dots are in each ten-frame. Write each number on the line. Then add the two numbers together.

____

+ ____

= ____
total

What number comes **before 11**?

What number comes **after 11**?

0 1 2 3 4 5 6 7 8 9 10 (11) 12 13 14 15 16 17 18 19 20

12

TWELVE

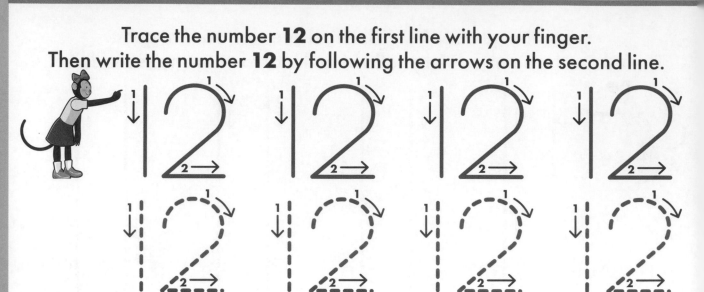

Trace the number **12** on the first line with your finger.
Then write the number **12** by following the arrows on the second line.

Count how many dots are in
each ten-frame. Write each
number on the line. Then add
the two numbers together.

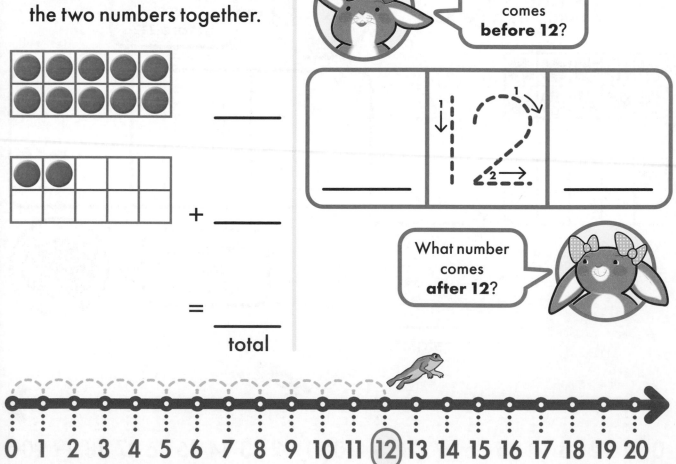

_____

+ _____

= _____
   total

What number
comes
before 12?

What number
comes
after 12?

0 1 2 3 4 5 6 7 8 9 10 11 (12) 13 14 15 16 17 18 19 20

13 THIRTEEN

Trace the number **13** on the first line with your finger.
Then write the number **13** by following the arrows on the second line.

Count how many dots are in each ten-frame. Write each number on the line. Then add the two numbers together.

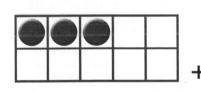

_____

+ _____

= _____
total

What number comes **before 13**?

What number comes **after 13**?

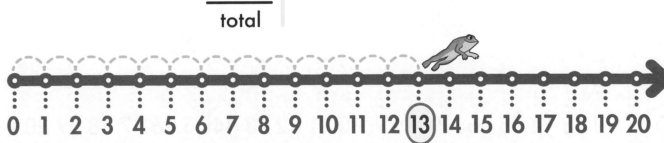

0 1 2 3 4 5 6 7 8 9 10 11 12 (13) 14 15 16 17 18 19 20

14

Trace the number **14** on the first line with your finger.
Then write the number **14** by following the arrows on the second line.

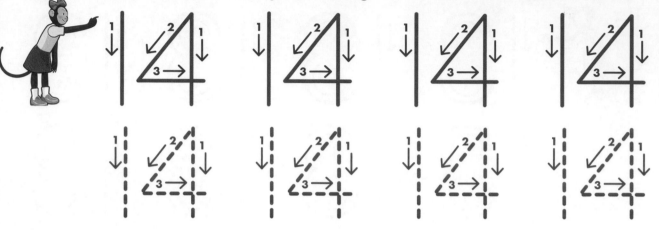

Count how many dots are in each ten-frame. Write each number on the line. Then add the two numbers together.

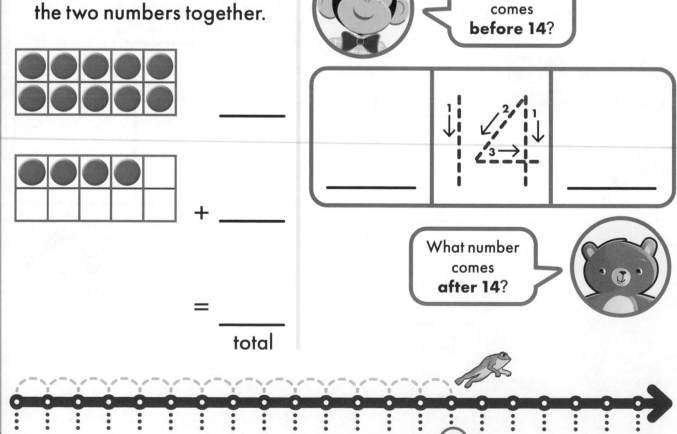

_____

+ _____

= _____
  total

What number comes **before 14**?

_____   _____

What number comes **after 14**?

0 1 2 3 4 5 6 7 8 9 10 11 12 13 (14) 15 16 17 18 19 20

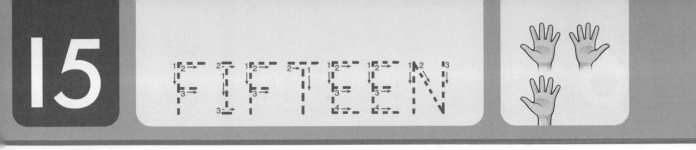

15

Trace the number **15** on the first line with your finger.
Then write the number **15** by following the arrows on the second line.

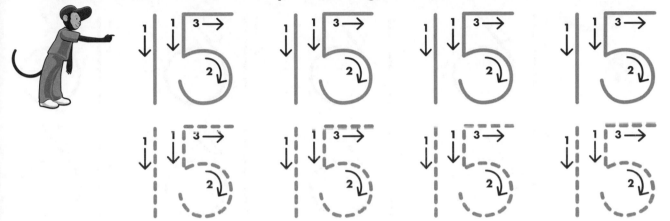

Count how many dots are in each ten-frame. Write each number on the line. Then add the two numbers together.

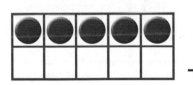

_____

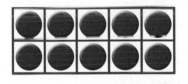

+ _____

= _____
total

What number comes **before 15**?

What number comes **after 15**?

0 1 2 3 4 5 6 7 8 9 10 11 12 13 14 (15) 16 17 18 19 20

16 SIXTEEN

Trace the number **16** on the first line with your finger.
Then write the number **16** by following the arrows on the second line.

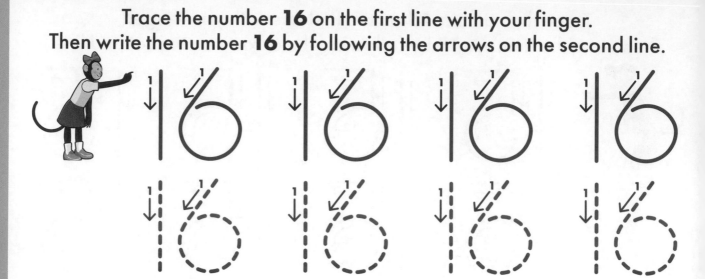

Count how many dots are in each ten-frame. Write each number on the line. Then add the two numbers together.

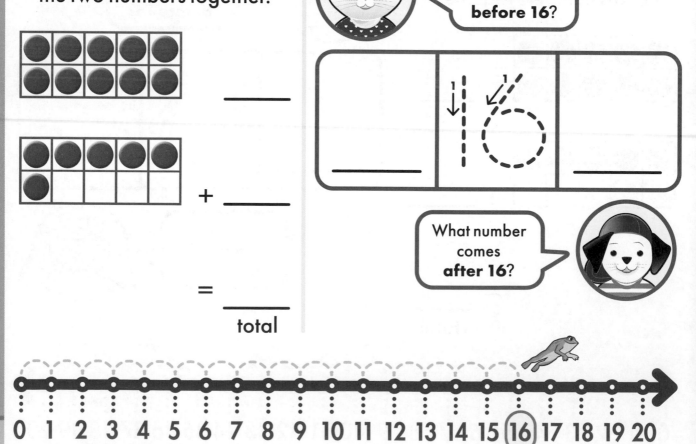

_____

+ _____

= _____
total

What number comes **before 16**?

What number comes **after 16**?

0 1 2 3 4 5 6 7 8 9 10 11 12 13 14 15 (16) 17 18 19 20

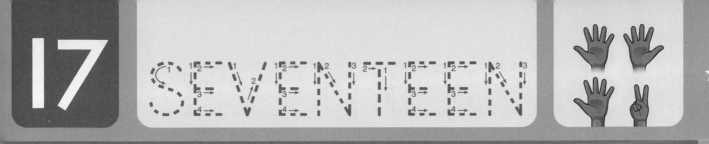
17

Trace the number **17** on the first line with your finger.
Then write the number **17** by following the arrows on the second line.

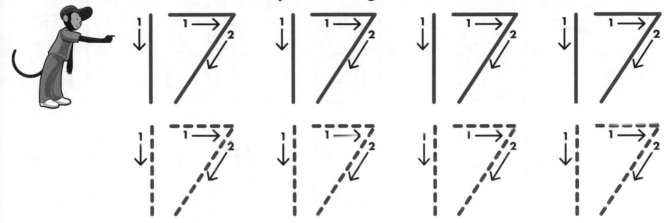

Count how many dots are in each ten-frame. Write each number on the line. Then add the two numbers together.

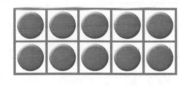

_____

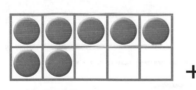

+ _____

= _____
total

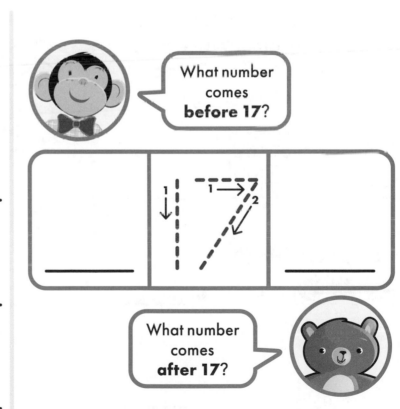

What number comes **before 17**?

What number comes **after 17**?

18

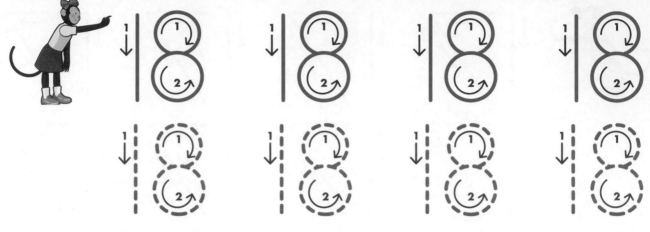

EIGHTEEN

Trace the number **18** on the first line with your finger.
Then write the number **18** by following the arrows on the second line.

Count how many dots are in each ten-frame. Write each number on the line. Then add the two numbers together.

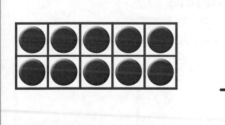

____

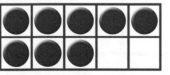

+ ____

= ____
total

What number comes **before 18**?

____   ____

What number comes **after 18**?

0 1 2 3 4 5 6 7 8 9 10 11 12 13 14 15 16 17 (18) 19 20

19 NINETEEN

Trace the number **19** on the first line with your finger.
Then write the number **19** by following the arrows on the second line.

Count how many dots are in each ten-frame. Write each number on the line. Then add the two numbers together.

_____

+ _____

= _____
total

What number comes **before 19**?

What number comes **after 19**?

0 1 2 3 4 5 6 7 8 9 10 11 12 13 14 15 16 17 18 (19) 20

20

Trace the number **20** on the first line with your finger.
Then write the number **20** by following the arrows on the second line.

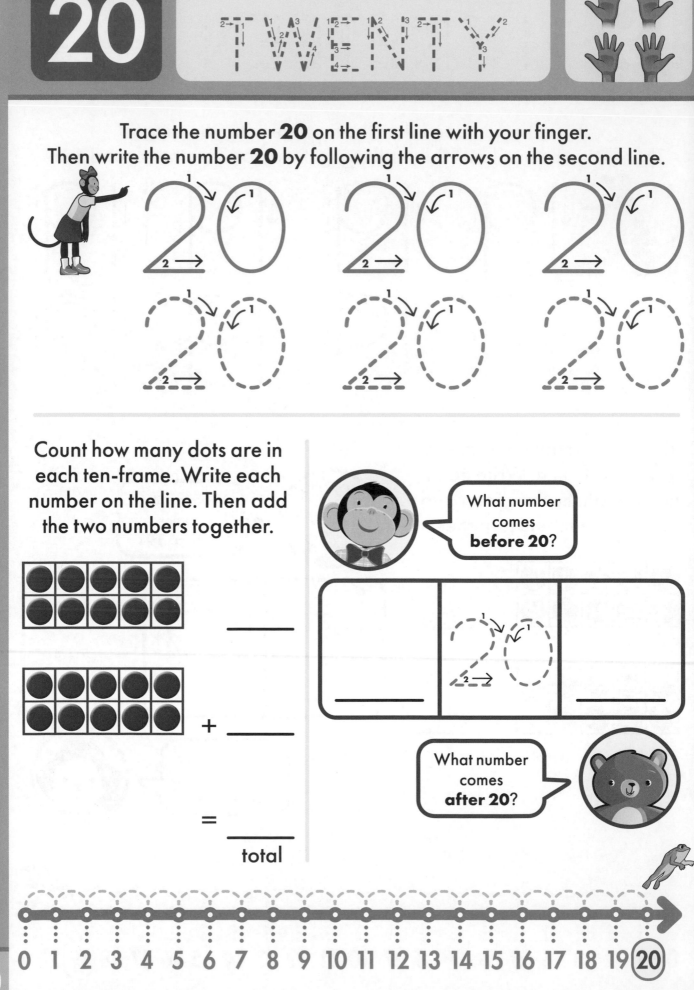

Count how many dots are in each ten-frame. Write each number on the line. Then add the two numbers together.

_____

+ _____

= _____
total

What number comes **before 20**?

_____   _____   _____

What number comes **after 20**?

0 1 2 3 4 5 6 7 8 9 10 11 12 13 14 15 16 17 18 19 20

Numbers 1–20

Trace the numbers that have been provided
and fill in the missing numbers.

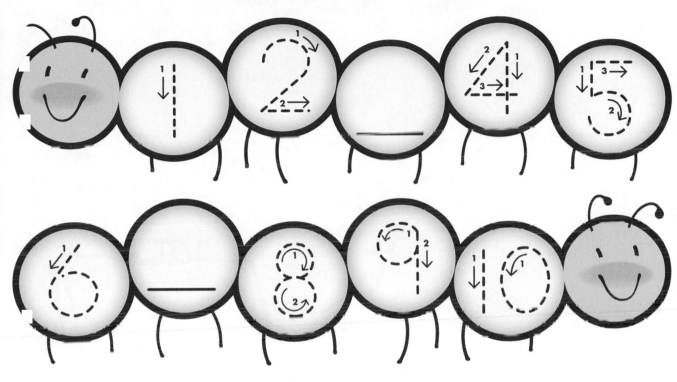

COLORS

I can trace the word yellow:

yellow   yellow

Count the yellow shapes. How many are there? _____

How many yellow rectangles do you see? _____

Put an X through all the shapes that are not yellow.

Color the flowers yellow. Then circle anything else in the picture that is yellow.

Find and color everything that can be yellow.

Blue

I can trace the word **blue**:

blue blue

Can you draw something that is **blue**?

Finish the pattern by coloring the white balloons **blue**. Say the pattern out loud when you're done.

Blue

Find and color everything that can be **blue**.

Red

I can trace the word **red**:

red   red

What am I? I am **red** but can also be green. I am shiny. I am crunchy. I taste sweet. What am I? Circle your answer!

How many **red** hearts are there? Circle the correct number.

3   4   5   6   7

Red

Find and color everything that can be **red**.

I can trace the word **green**:

green   green

Count the green shapes. How many are there? _____

How many green triangles do you see? _____

Put an X through all the shapes that are not green.

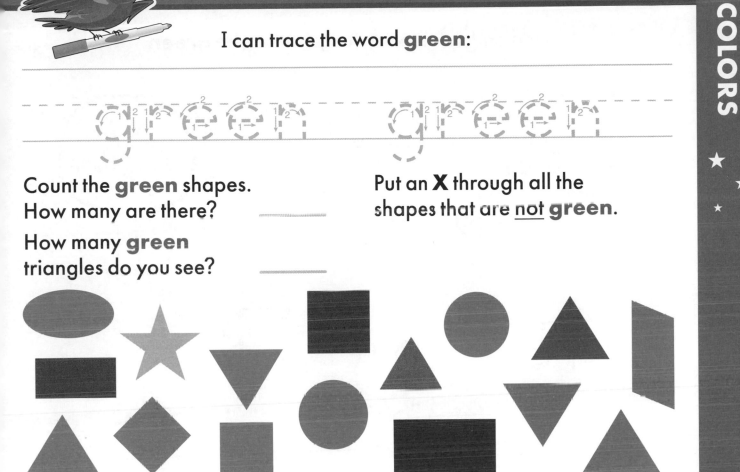

What am I? I am green. I can hop. I eat flies. I say ribbit. What am I? Circle your answer!

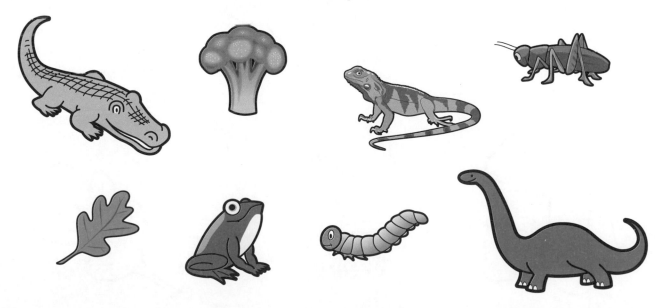

Green

Find and color everything that can be **green**.

Black

I can trace the word **black**:

black black

Color the cars **black**. Then circle anything else in the picture that is **black**.

Can you draw something that is **black**?

Black

Find and color everything that can be **black**.

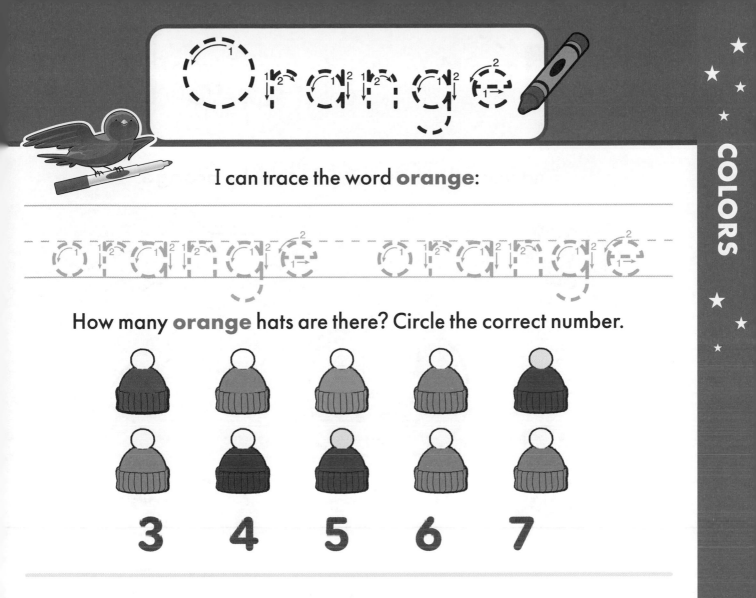

I can trace the word orange:

How many orange hats are there? Circle the correct number.

3   4   5   6   7

Color the pumpkin **orange**. Then draw a face to make a jack-o'-lantern.

Orange

Find and color everything that can be **orange**.

Purple

I can trace the word **purple**:

purple purple

Finish the pattern by coloring the white fish **purple**.
Say the pattern out loud when you're done.

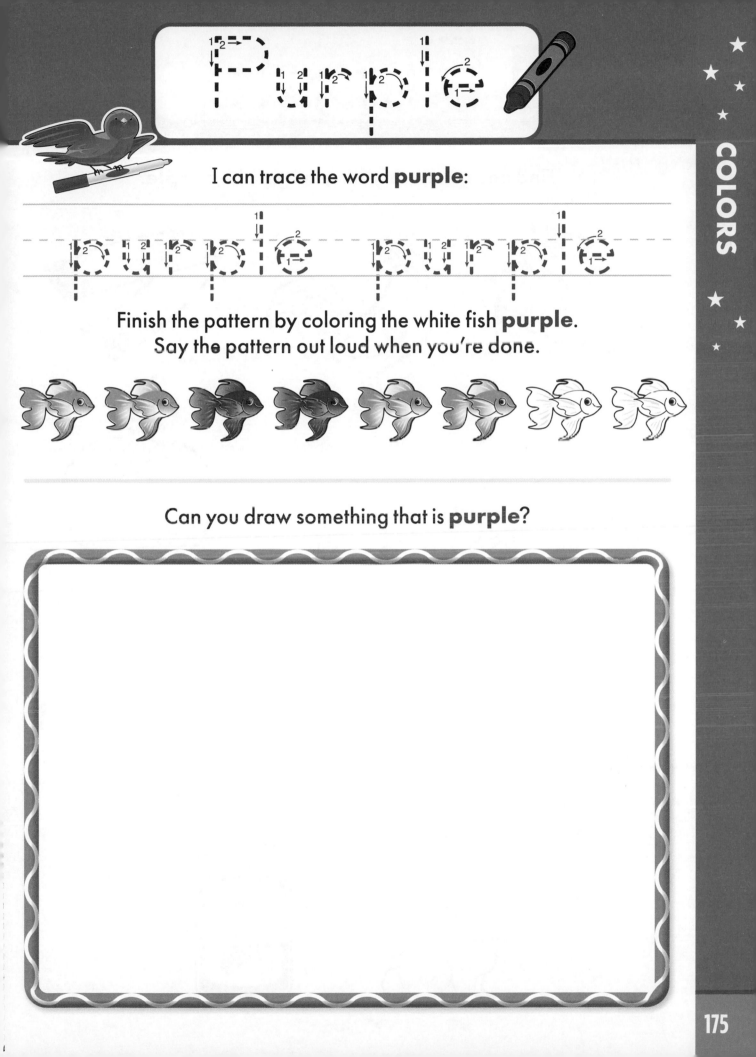

Can you draw something that is **purple**?

175

Purple

Find and color everything that can be **purple**.

Pink

I can trace the word **pink**:

pink   pink

Finish the pattern by coloring the white ice cream cones **pink**.
Say the pattern out loud when you're done.

How many **pink** flowers are there? Circle the correct number.

3   4   5   6   7

Pink

Find and color everything that can be **pink**.

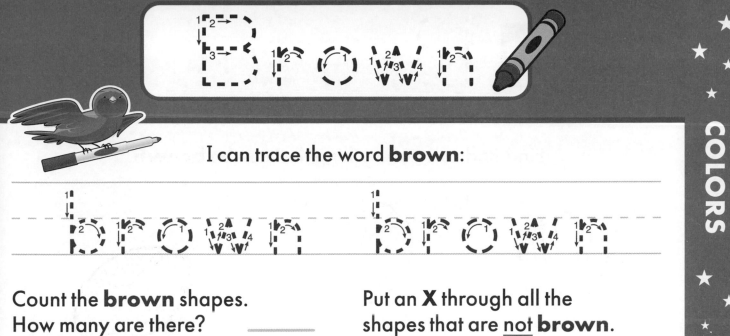

I can trace the word **brown**:

brown brown

Count the **brown** shapes. How many are there? _____

How many **brown** circles do you see? _____

Put an **X** through all the shapes that are not **brown**.

Color the monkey **brown**. Then circle anything in the picture that is **brown**.

Brown

Find and color everything that can be **brown**.

White

I can trace the word white :

white   white

What am I? I am white . I make you smile. I am pretty.
You never see me in the summer. I fall from the sky.
What am I? Circle your answer!

Sidewalk CHALK

Count the white shapes.
How many are there? _____

How many white
squares do you see? _____

Put an **X** through all the
shapes that are <u>not</u> white .

White

Find and color everything that can be white.

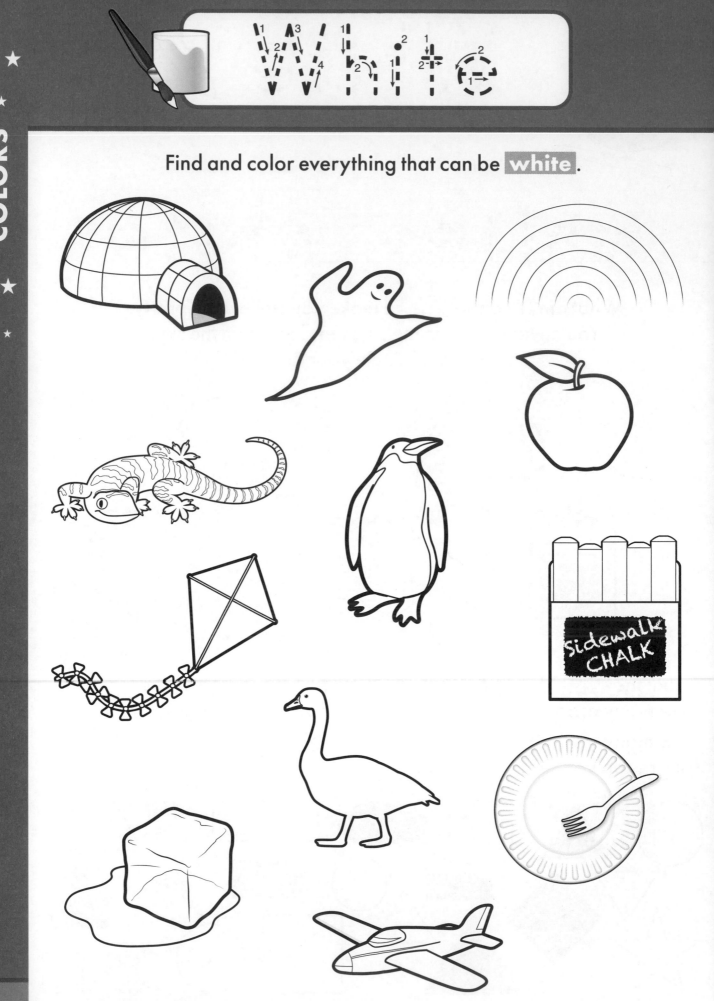

SHAPES

▲ Triangle ▲

A **triangle** has three sides.
Practice drawing **triangles** by tracing the **triangles** below.

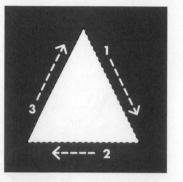

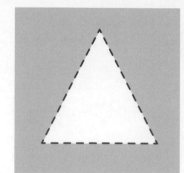

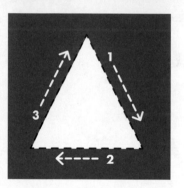

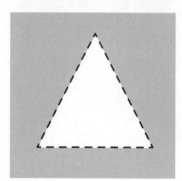

Trace the word **triangle**.

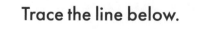

Trace the line below.

▲ Triangle ▲

Help Jenny find the soccer ball by following the **triangles**.

▲ Triangle ▲

Circle the **triangle** that is the same as the first **triangle** in each row.

There are seven **triangles** below. Color each **triangle purple**.

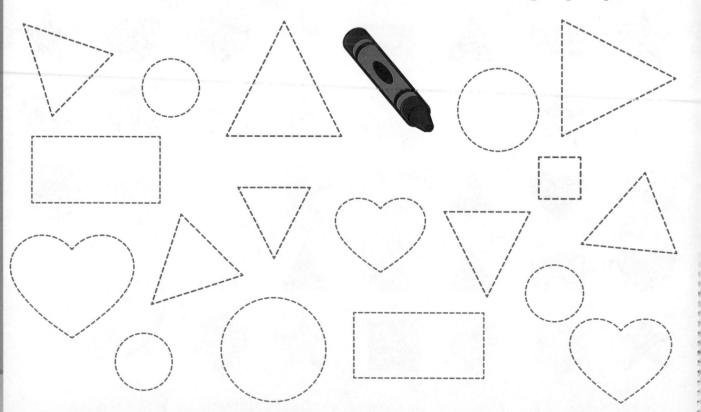

★ Star ★

Trace the **stars**.

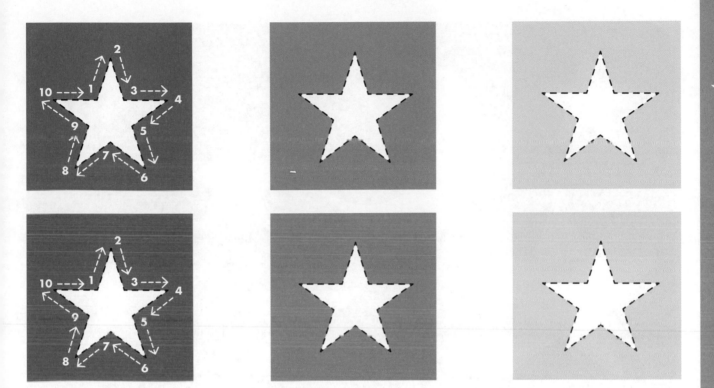

Trace the word **star**.

Follow the steps below to draw your own **star**.

★ Star ★

Trace the **stars** below and color them.

Color the last **star** to complete the pattern.

★ Star ★

Connect the dots from 1 to 10 to 1 to see
the shape below. Color it **orange**.

3

5•   •4   2•   •1

•6   10•

8

7•   •9

Help the horse find its barn by following the **stars**.

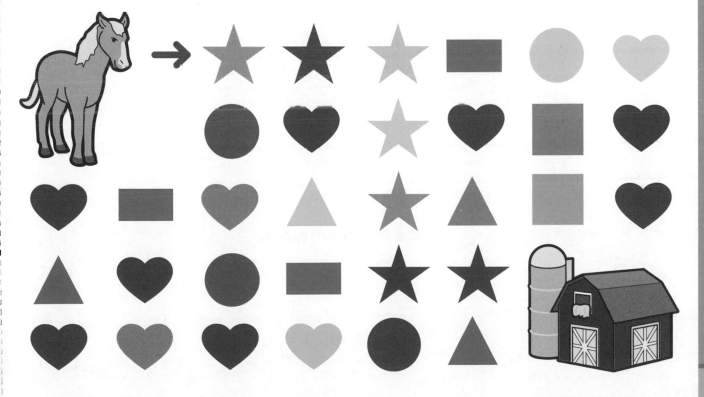

● Circle ●

A **circle** is round.
Practice drawing **circles** by tracing the circles below.

Trace the word **circle**.

Trace the line below.

● Circle ●

Trace the **circles** and then color them, each in a different color.

Use the numbers to fill in the picture. What do you **see**?
Can you also see the **circles**?
1 = **purple** 2 = yellow

● Circle ●

Trace the **circles**. Draw a hat and arms on the snowman.

Color the last **circle** to complete the pattern.

Square

A **square** has four equal sides.
Practice drawing **squares** by tracing the **squares** below.

Trace the word **square**.

Trace the line below.

Square

Color the **squares** that are the same size.

Connect the dots with a **blue** crayon to make as many **squares** as you can. The first one has been done for you.

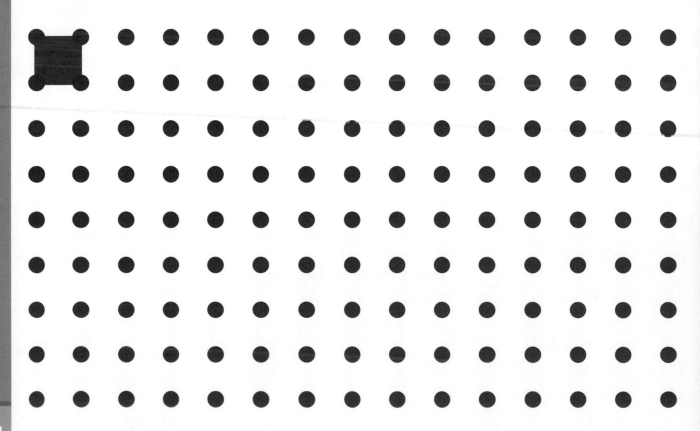

Square

Trace the **square** windows on the school bus.

What is fun to open that is **square**?
Connect the dots to find out.

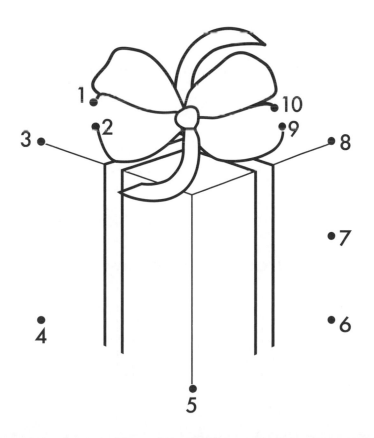

Rectangle

A **rectangle** has four sides. Two sides are long. Two sides are short. Practice drawing **rectangles** by tracing the **rectangles** below.

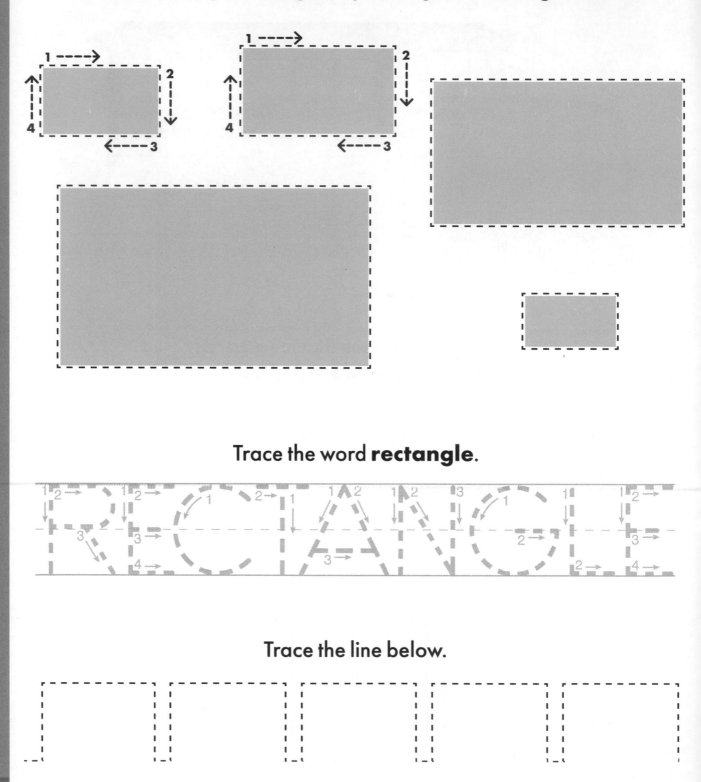

Trace the word **rectangle**.

Trace the line below.

Help the rabbit get to its carrot by following the **rectangles**.

Rectangle

Rectangles can come in all different sizes.
Find and circle five **rectangles** below.

Oval

Practice drawing **ovals** by tracing the **ovals** below.

Trace the word **oval**.

Trace the line below.

SHAPES ★

199

Oval

Trace the **oval** spots on the cow and color them **black**.

Circle the **oval** that is the same as the first **oval** in each row.

Trace the **ovals** in the cheese below.

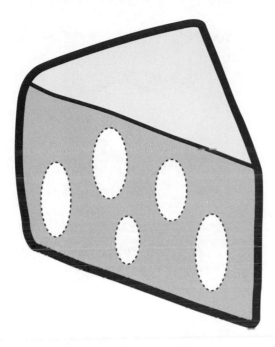

Help the dentist get to the tooth by following the path of **ovals**.

♥ Heart ♥

Practice drawing **hearts** by tracing the dotted lines below.

Trace the word **heart**.

Trace the line below.

♥ Heart ♥

Help the chicken get to its chick through the **heart** maze.

Color the last shape to complete the color pattern.

♥ Heart ♥

Use the numbers to fill in the picture below.
What do you see? Can you see the **heart**?
1 = **red** 2 = **black** 3 = **blue**

Diamond

Practice drawing **diamonds** by tracing the dotted lines below.

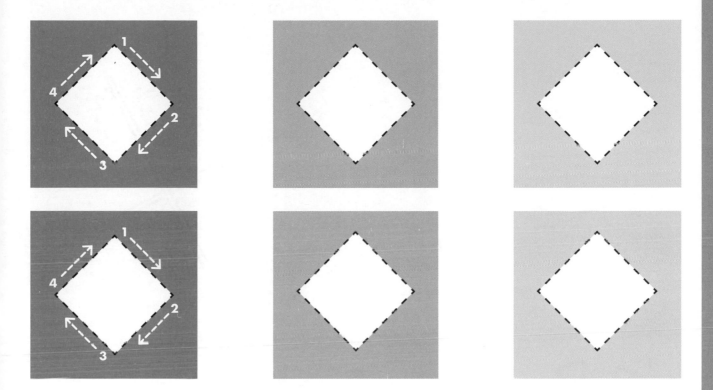

Trace the word **diamond**.

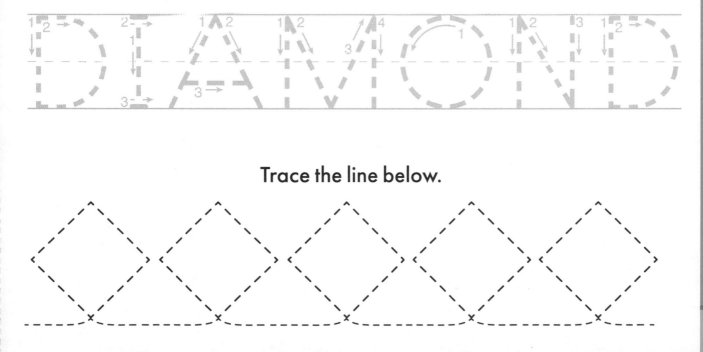

Trace the line below.

◆ Diamond ◆

Trace the **diamond** shape and then color the kite.

Color the last shape to complete the pattern.

Diamond

Help the mail carrier deliver mail through the **diamond** maze.

Color the seven **diamonds** below green.

SCIENCE

The Five Senses

Finish each sentence by tracing words for **the five senses**.

feel   hear   smell   see   taste

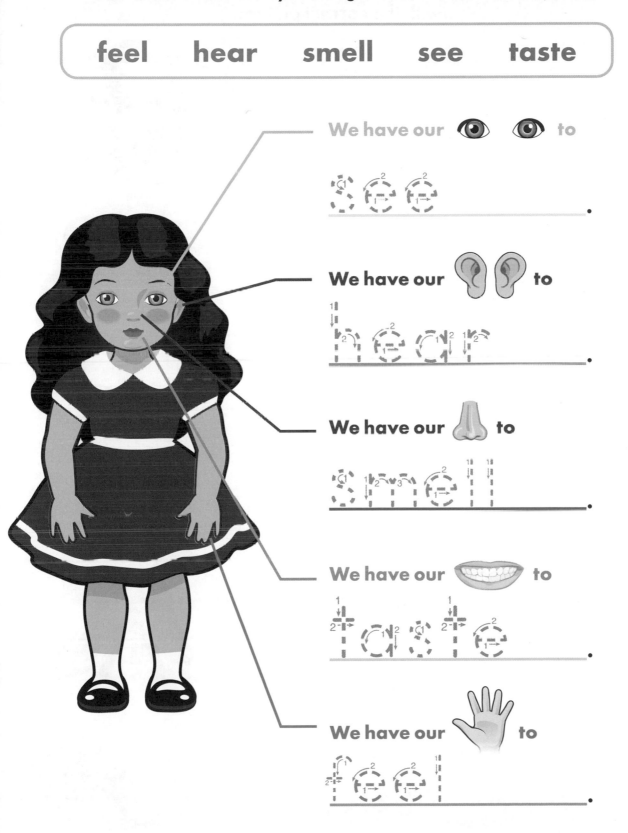

We have our 👁 👁 to

s e e .

We have our 👂 to

h e a r .

We have our 👃 to

s m e l l .

We have our 👄 to

t a s t e .

We have our ✋ to

f e e l .

209

The Five Senses

Draw a line that matches each of **the five senses** with the correct picture.

See

Smell

Taste

Feel

Hear

The Five Senses

Our nose  is the part of our body that helps us smell. Some things we smell we might like and some things we might not like!

Look at each picture below.
Circle the happy face if you like the smell.
Circle the unhappy face if you do NOT like the smell.

😊 like   🙁 do not like

😊 like   🙁 do not like

😊 like   🙁 do not like

😊 like   🙁 do not like

😊 like   🙁 do not like

😊 like   🙁 do not like

😊 like   🙁 do not like

😊 like   🙁 do not like

😊 like   🙁 do not like

211

The Five Senses

Our eyes 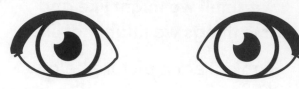 are parts of the body that help us see.
What color are your eyes? Color the eyes to match your own:

Think about taking a walk on a cold winter day.
What are some things you might see? Draw two things below.

Think about taking a walk on a warm summer day.
What are some things you might see? Draw two things below.

The Five Senses

Our ears 👂👂 are parts of the body that help us hear.

Look at each picture below and think about what it sounds like.
Circle the loud face if you think it is loud.
Circle the quiet face if you think it is quiet.

Loud   Quiet

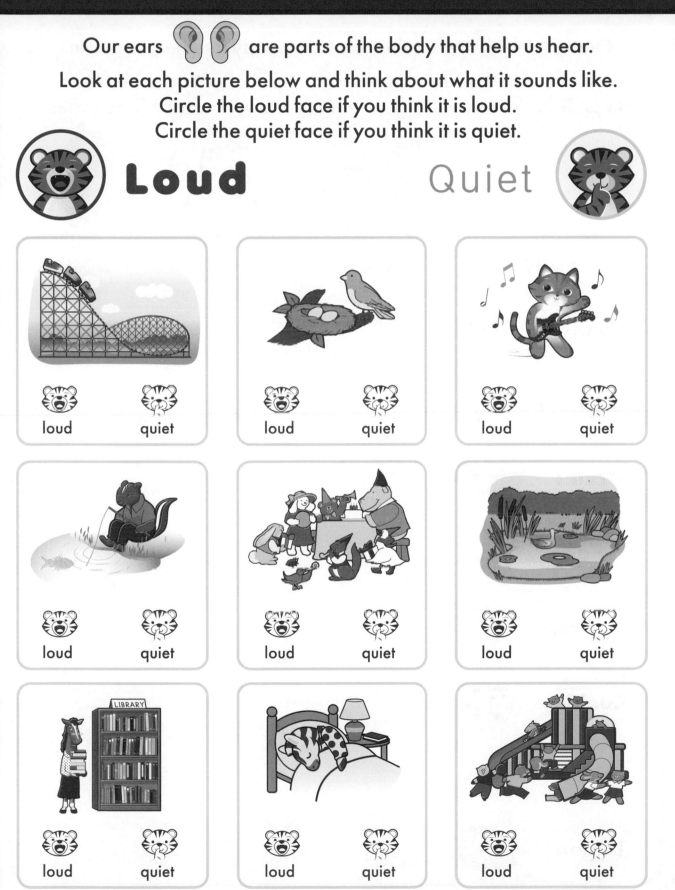

loud   quiet

loud   quiet

loud   quiet

loud   quiet

loud   quiet

loud   quiet

loud   quiet

loud   quiet

loud   quiet

213

The Five Senses

Our mouth  is the part of the body that helps us taste.

Look at each of the foods below and think about how they taste.
Put an **X** under sweet, salty, or sour to show how each food tastes.

Food	Sweet	Salty	Sour
Chips			
Ice Cream			
Pickles			
Banana			
French Fries			
Cookie			
Pizza			
Lemon			

The Five Senses

Our hands  are parts of the body that help us feel.

Look around your house for something that feels smooth, rough, hard, soft, sticky, and scratchy. Draw them below.

Smooth

Rough

Hard

Scratchy

Sticky

Soft

215

Don't Litter

Littering is against the law. It can hurt animals.
It is important to clean up your garbage.
No one wants to be a litterbug! Color the sign below.

Don't Be a
Litterbug

Help Keep Our Planet Clean!

Circle all of the things that do not belong in nature.

Reduce, Reuse, Recycle

To **reduce** is to try to throw less trash away.
To **reuse** is to try to get new uses from things.
If you no longer need or want something, pass it on!
To **recycle** is to take something old, make it new, and use it again.

Look at the items below. Help **recycle** them by sorting them
and drawing a line from each one to the correct **recycle** bin.

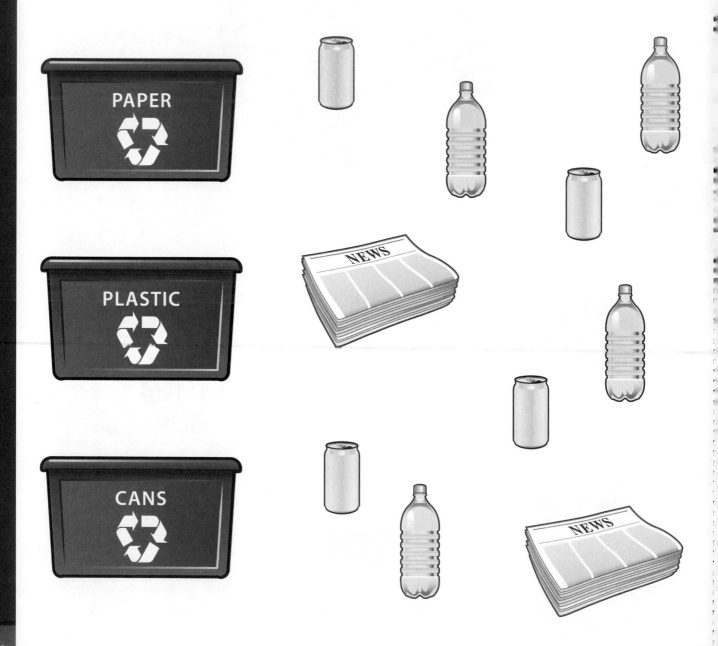

Reduce, Reuse, Recycle

Help the newspaper find its way through the maze to its recycle bin.

PAPER

Seasons: Winter

Trace the word **winter**.

winter winter

During the **winter**, it gets very cold.
It can even snow! Circle the clothes that you
would wear in the **winter**.

Draw a picture of your favorite thing to do in the **winter**.
Is it playing in the snow, going ice-skating, or enjoying
a cup of hot chocolate with marshmallows?

Seasons: Spring

Trace the word **spring**.

spring   spring

During the **spring**, the snow has melted, and it is starting to warm up outside. **Spring** showers bring lots of rain! Circle the clothes that you would wear in the **spring**.

Draw a picture of your favorite thing to do in the **spring**. Is it jumping in rain puddles, planting a garden, or playing outside?

221

Seasons: Summer

Trace the word **summer**.

summer summer

During the **summer**, it gets very hot.
It is a good time to go to the beach! Circle the clothes
that you would wear in the **summer**.

Draw a picture of your favorite thing to do in the **summer**.
Is it playing outside all day, going swimming,
or meeting friends at the park?

Seasons: Fall

Trace the word **fall**.

fall   fall

During the **fall**, it is starting to get colder. The leaves start
falling off the trees, and it gets dark earlier!
Circle the clothes that you would wear in the **fall**.

Draw a picture of your favorite thing to do in the **fall**.
Is it playing in the leaves, getting ready for
Halloween, or sitting by a campfire?

223

Seasons

Trace the words for each season. Then decorate
each tree, showing how it would look for each season.

Seasons

Finish the pattern by circling the correct answer.

summer   fall

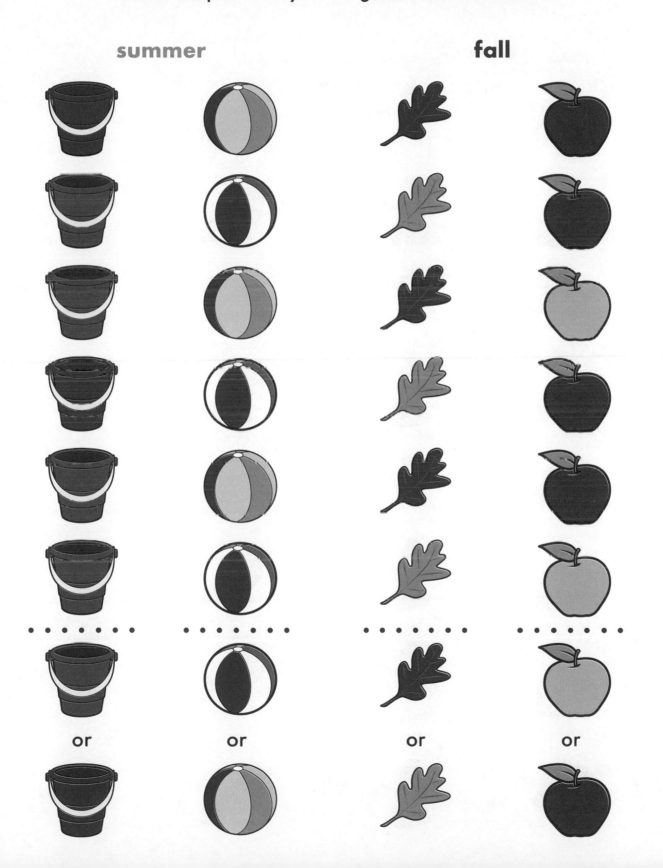

Seasons

Finish the pattern by circling the correct answer.

winter

spring

or **or** **or** **or**

Is It Hot or Is It Cold?

Look at the picture. If you think the weather is **hot**, trace the word **hot**. If you think it is **cold**, trace the word **cold**.

Weather

Look at each picture and draw a line to the kind of weather it shows.

Today's Weather

Go outside and take a minute to notice how the weather is where you live. Then answer the questions.

Today's temperature feels (trace the correct word below):

hot   warm   cold

Circle today's matching precipitation. Today's precipitation is:

dry   **rainy**   **snowy**

A **prediction** is when you guess what you think might happen. What do you **predict** the weather will be like tomorrow? Circle your **prediction** below:

sunny	cloudy
rainy	snowing
windy	stormy

hot

°F   °C
120   50
100   40
80   30
60   20
40   10
20   0
0   -10
-20   -20
-40   -30
   -40

warm

°F   °C
120   50
100   40
80   30
60   20
40   10
20   0
0   -10
-20   -20
-40   -30
   -40

cold

°F   °C
120   50
100   40
80   30
60   20
40   10
20   0
0   -10
-20   -20
-40   -30
   -40

Life Cycle of Plants

Flowers grow from seeds. Label the drawings from 1 to 4 to show the plant life cycle. Color the flower when you are done.

Parts of Plants

Label the parts of a flower using the words below.

roots   stem   leaf   petals

Color the roots 🖍 .

Color the stem 🖍 .

Color the leaves 🖍 .

Color the petals any color you like!

231

Life Cycle of Plants

How do tomatoes grow? Number the steps in order
from 1 to 4, from planting seeds to watering the plants,
picking the tomatoes, and eating them.

Farm Animals

Circle all of the animals that you might find on a farm.

Ocean Animals

Color all of the animals that might live in the ocean.

Are You My Mommy?

Draw a line from the mama to her baby.

Fly or Swim?

Draw a line from each animal to the sky if it can fly or to the sea if it can swim.

Animals and Their Sounds

Draw a line from the animal to the sound it makes.

oink

chirp

moo

meow

bark

ribbit

roar

Animals and Their Homes

Draw a line from the animal to its home.

BASIC CONCEPTS

Circle the two pictures that are the **same** in each row.

Same

Draw a line connecting the three pairs of flowers that match.

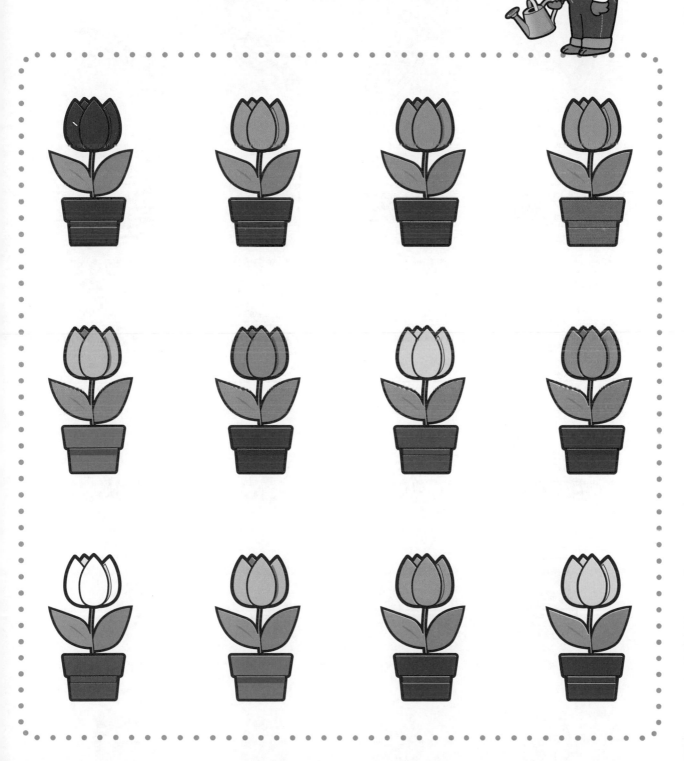

Different

Circle the picture that is **different** in each row.

Different

Find and circle five differences between the top picture and the bottom picture.

Opposites

Look at the pictures below and draw a line connecting each picture on the left to its **opposite** on the right. The first one is done for you.

asleep — short

long — full

empty — awake

day — dry

small — night

wet — large

Opposites

Look at the pictures below and draw a line connecting each picture on the left to its **opposite** on the right.

front

slow

weak

happy

clean

hot

fast

strong

back

cold

sad

dirty

Differences

Circle the object that is **biggest**.

Big   **Bigger**   **Biggest**

Circle the object that is **smallest**.

Small   **Smaller**   **Smallest**

Circle the object that is **softest**.

Soft   **Softer**   **Softest**

Differences

Circle the object that is **tallest**.

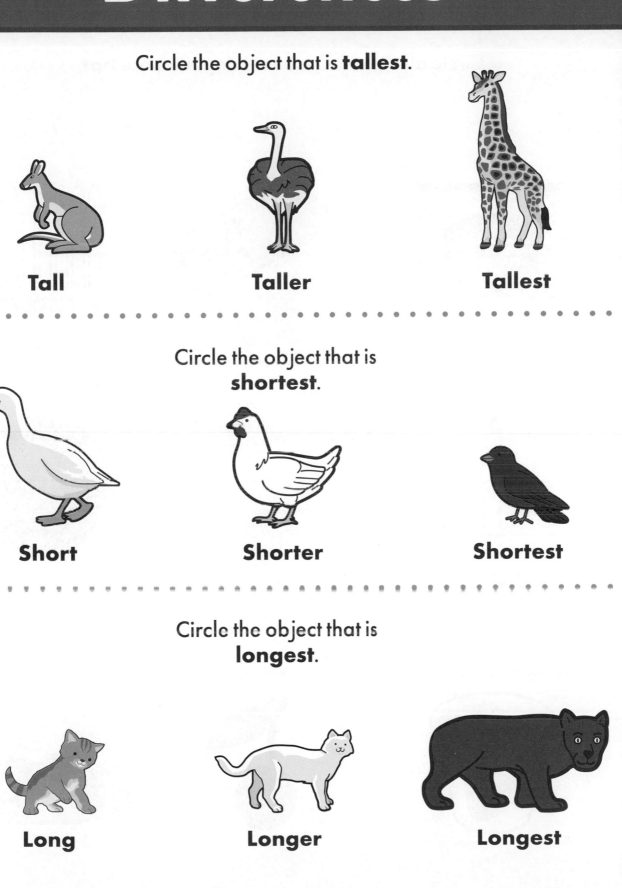

Tall

Taller

Tallest

Circle the object that is
shortest.

Short

Shorter

Shortest

Circle the object that is
longest.

Long

Longer

Longest

What Is Hot?

Circle all of the pictures of things that are **hot**.

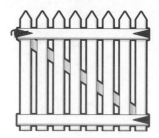

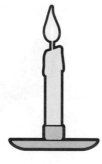

What Is Cold?

Circle all of the pictures of things that are **cold**.

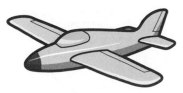

Directions

Children are playing at the playground. Find the children who are on the **top** and **bottom** of the green slide. Circle them in blue.

Look for the two kids who are **in** and **out** of the yellow slide. Circle them in red, as well as the two kids who are **on** and **off** the stairs.

Color the ball in the **middle**.

Color the ball on the **bottom**.

Color the ball on the **top**.

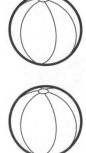

Directions

Two kids are playing on the monkey bars. One is **over** the bars.
The other is **under**. Circle the one who is **over** the bars in blue.

Two kids are playing on the seesaw. One kid is **high**.
The other is **low**. Circle the one who is **low** in red.

Where is the fox?
Circle the words that describe where the fox is in relation to the box.

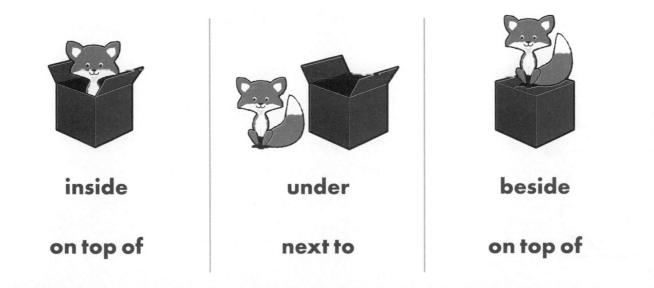

inside	**under**	**beside**
on top of	**next to**	**on top of**

251

Left

Touch your hand to the handprint. This is your **LEFT** hand.

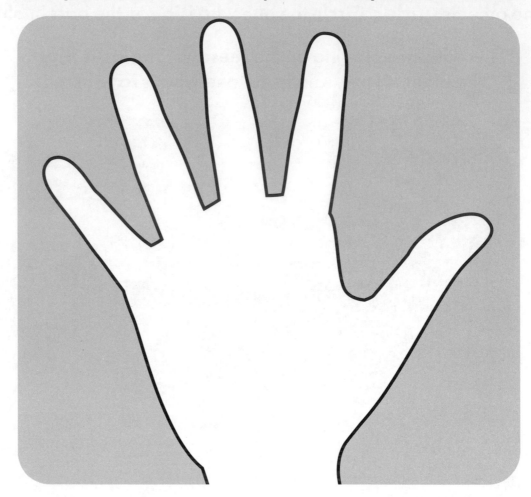

Have a grown-up read the following directions
to you and see how well you do!

Raise your left foot.

Touch your right ear.

Raise your left hand.

Turn your head
to the right.

Touch your left elbow.

Stomp your right foot.

Touch your right eye.

Touch your left ankle.

Bend your right knee.

Right

Touch your hand to the handprint. This is your **RIGHT** hand.

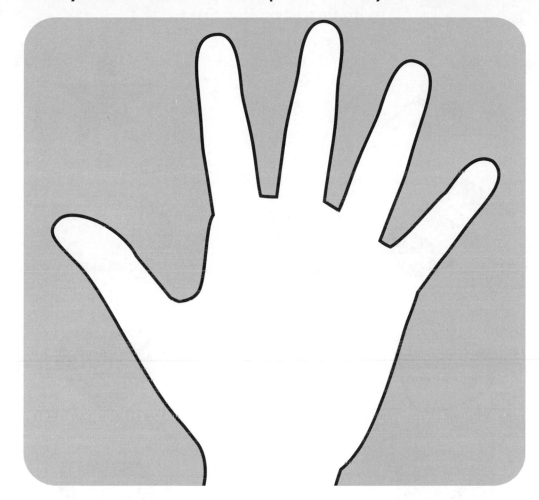

Circle the fish that are swimming to the **right**.
Draw an **X** through the fish that are swimming to the **left**.

Match the Picture to Its Shape

Draw a line to match the picture on the left to its shape on the right.

Things That Go Together

Draw a line between the things that go together.

Things That Go Together

Draw a line between the things that go together.

What's Wrong with This Picture?

Circle everything that does not belong in the sky.
There are five things.

Circle everything that does not belong in the ocean.
There are six things.

Rhyming

Look at the first picture in each row.
Circle the picture to the right that rhymes with it.

Rhyming

Draw a line to match each picture on the left
with its rhyming partner on the right.

car

goat

house

cat

rain

clock

hat

mouse

train

star

boat

block

ALL ABOUT ME

My Portrait

Finish the picture to create your own portrait.

My name is: _____.

All About Me

Color your answers below.

The color of my eyes is...

The color of my hair is...

My favorite color is...

I am ⬭ years old.

Happy Birthday!

I am this old

1 2 3 4 5 6 7

The day my birthday falls on is

1	2	3	4	5	6	7
8	9	10	11	12	13	14
15	16	17	18	19	20	21
22	23	24	25	26	27	28
29	30	31				

Draw how many candles you need.

Color in the cupcake that shows the month of your birthday.

January   February   March   April   May   June   July   August   September   October   November   December

All About Me

Some of my favorite foods are:

My favorite sports are:

Draw a picture of your family.

My Phone Number

It is important for you to know your phone number.
Practice repeating it often so you don't forget it!

I know my home phone number:

___ ___ ___ - ___ ___ ___ - ___ ___ ___ ___

I know these important cell numbers:

___ ___ ___ - ___ ___ ___ - ___ ___ ___ ___

___ ___ ___ - ___ ___ ___ - ___ ___ ___ ___

Use your fingers to call your phone number.

All About Me

All About Me

I can trace my handprints.

Right Hand

I can trace my right hand.

When I grow up I want to be...

Emotions

Draw a face to go with each emotion.

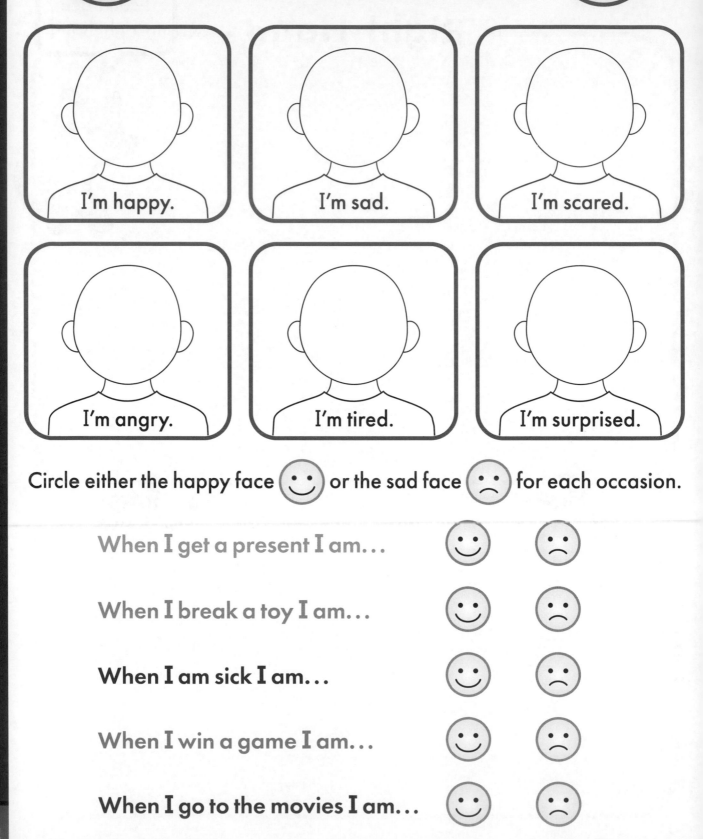

I'm happy.

I'm sad.

I'm scared.

I'm angry.

I'm tired.

I'm surprised.

Circle either the happy face 😊 or the sad face 🙁 for each occasion.

When I get a present I am…

When I break a toy I am…

When I am sick I am…

When I win a game I am…

When I go to the movies I am…

Good Night's Sleep

Zippy the Zebra needs to get a good night's sleep for school tomorrow. Help Zippy get ready by numbering the boxes 1 to 4 to show the right order to follow for going to bed.

Getting Ready for School

You have to get ready for school!
Number the boxes below in the right order from 1 to 4.

What Will You Need?

Circle all of the things you might need to pack in your backpack for school.

Inside and Outside Voices

Color the pictures below.

| This is my inside voice.
It is quiet. | This is my outside voice.
It is loud! |

Look at the pictures below. Draw a circle around
inside voice if you use a quiet voice, or
outside voice if you use a loud voice.

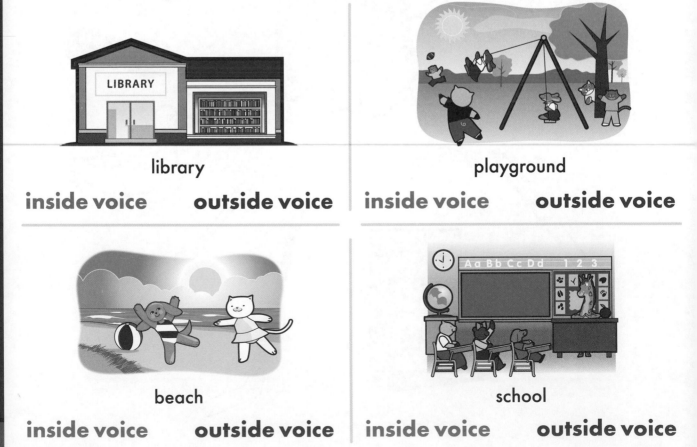

library

inside voice   **outside voice**

playground

inside voice   **outside voice**

beach

inside voice   **outside voice**

school

inside voice   **outside voice**

Tattling vs. Reporting

Sometimes people do things we don't like.
Before you tell an adult, think. Are you tattling or reporting?

Have someone read you the descriptions below to help you learn the difference between tattling and reporting.

Tattling

- Usually means you're trying to get someone in trouble
- Means going to an adult with a problem that you can probably solve on your own
- Means going to an adult about something that is not very important

Reporting

- Means that you're trying to keep someone safe
- Means going to an adult because you need help
- Means you're not trying to get anyone in trouble, you just want to help
- Means something important has happened and an adult needs to know

Have someone read the sentences to you.
If you think it is **tattling**, color the speech bubble **red**.
If you think it is **reporting**, color the speech bubble **blue**.

Kaitlyn took my blue crayon.

An older kid is picking on a classmate.

Patrick pushed me really hard down on the ground.

A friend fell and is bleeding.

A friend said something hurtful.

Someone scribbled on my paper.

Someone in class is being very bossy.

Someone threw a rock at someone else.

Taking Turns

We let our friends play with our toys. We play with their toys.
When we are done, we give them back. This is **sharing**.

not sharing

sharing

I can share my **ball**.

I can take turns on the **swings**.

I can take turns playing a **game**.

I can share my **crayon**.

Taking Turns

Taking turns isn't always easy. When you don't share or take turns, you can make someone feel bad.

Circle how would you feel if someone didn't give you a turn with a toy?

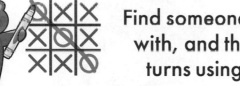 Find someone to play tic-tac-toe with, and then practice taking turns using the grids below.

Please and Thank You

Saying **please** shows that you are asking nicely.
When you ask for something, it is polite to say **please**.

Say **thank you** when a friend does or gives you something.
If a friend offers you something, you say **yes, please**,
or **no, thank you**.

If you need a friend to pass you a crayon,
what should you say?
Trace the letters.

PLEASE

After a friend passes you a crayon, what should you say?
Trace the letters.

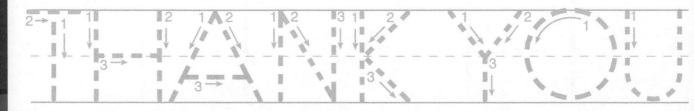

THANK YOU

Please and Thank You

Draw a line from the object to either **please**, if you would like to eat it, or **no, thank you**, if you would not like to eat it.

please

no, thank you

Rules at School

Talk with an adult about how you should act at school
and then color the pictures.

I can walk quietly in the hallway.

I can sit quietly on the carpet.

I can work with others.

I can raise my hand to speak.

I can take care of supplies.

I can try my best!

Library

When you go to the library, the librarian can help you pick out books you will like. Draw the cover of your favorite book.

Saying I'm Sorry

Saying you're **sorry** is called apologizing. When you apologize, you're telling another person that you feel bad for the pain you caused, even if you didn't do it on purpose.

Draw a line from **I'm sorry** to the reasons you should say **I'm sorry**.

Giving a parent a present.

Breaking
a friend's toy.

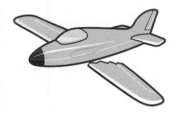

Saying something
mean.

I'm Sorry

Calling a classmate
a bad name.

Telling a friend you
like them.

Opening a door for
a teacher.

Saying Excuse Me

Saying **excuse me** is good manners.
When should you say **excuse me**?
Answer **yes** or **no** to the following situations.

When you bump into a teacher?

yes no

When you play ball with a friend?

yes no

When you need to get the librarian's attention?

yes no

**When you did not hear or understand
what a classmate said?**

yes no

When you read a book?

yes no

When you burp?

yes no

When you sleep?

yes no

281

Saying Excuse Me

Color the picture of the skunk saying **excuse me** for knocking down his friend.

Be Kind to Others

Be kind to others by treating them the way you want to be treated. Draw a line from each action to either **kind** or **unkind**.

kind

unkind

Asking a classmate to play with you.

Pushing a friend down.

Waiting in line to take a turn.

Picking up a book for a friend who drops it.

Getting mad at a friend.

Not allowing a classmate to play with you.

Letting a friend borrow your crayons.

Be Kind to Others

If you saw a friend who was crying because no one would play with her, what would you do?
Draw a picture to show how you would **be kind**.

MY WORLD

Stop, Look, and Listen

Before we cross any street we have to
stop, **look**, and **listen!**

Draw a line from each word to its matching picture.

STOP

LOOK

LISTEN

Traffic Lights

The color of a traffic light tells cars what to do. **Red** means stop, yellow means slow down and look for cars, and **green** means go. Color the traffic light and trace the words below.

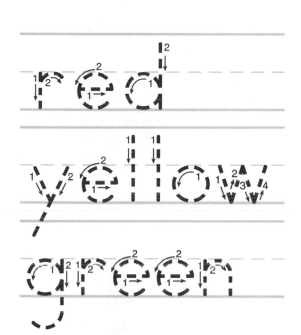

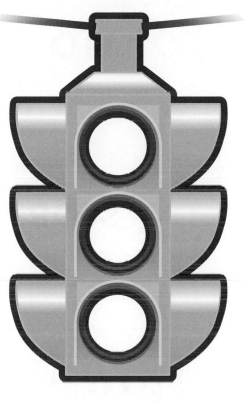

Traffic Safety

Draw a line between the traffic light color and what it means.

GO

STOP

SLOW DOWN

Stop Signs

A **stop sign** is **red** with white letters.
It has a white border and eight sides.
When you see it on a street, you should **stop**.

Connect the dots from 1 to 8 to 1 to complete
the **stop sign** below. Then color it.

Car Safety

Circle the correct way to ride in a car.

Helmet Safety

You always need to wear a **helmet** when you're on a bike, a skateboard, or a scooter.

Helmets are important for safety. Draw a line from the boy with the **helmet** to activities where he must wear a **helmet**.

riding a skateboard

riding in a car

riding a bike

playing basketball

riding a scooter

playing hopscotch

going to the dentist

291

Important People

Circle the people whose job it is to care for others.

Workers and Their Tools

Draw a line from each person to the object they use at work.

CRAFTS

Cute Caterpillar

Let's make a **green** caterpillar! Follow the dotted lines to cut out the caterpillar's face and body. Tape the six strips into links and the caterpillar's face to the first link.

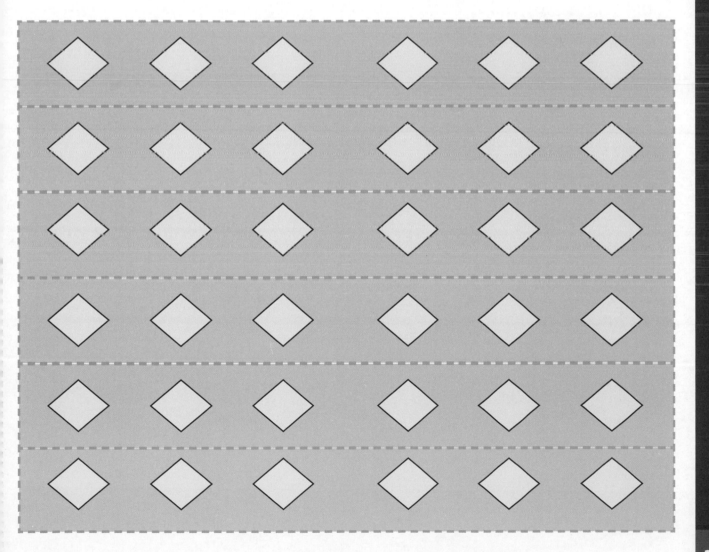

Beautiful Butterfly!

Cut along the outside of the art, following the arrows. Fold the wings along the dotted line. Attach a Popsicle stick to the back of the butterfly's body to make a puppet.

Larry the Lion

Cut the lion's head out by following the line along the mane.
Cut the lines in the mane to make fringe.

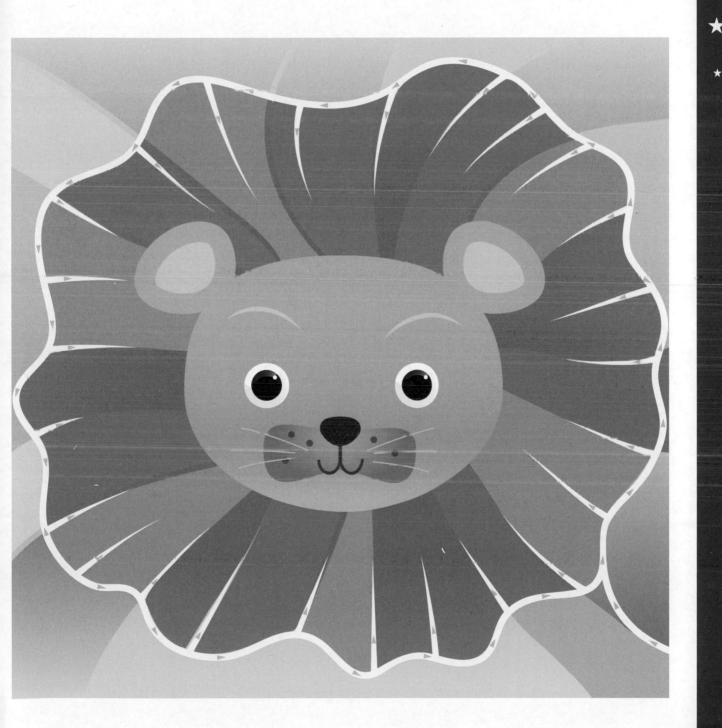

Dragonfly

Cut along the arrows on the outside of the art. Fold along the dotted lines so the dragonfly's wings flap. Tape or glue a Popsicle stick to the back of the body to make it into a puppet!

Jaguar in a Traveling Cage

Cut along the arrows around the cage below. Fold up along the dotted line at the bottom of the bars. Use four pieces of tape to attach the sides. **Now you have a jaguar in a traveling cage!**

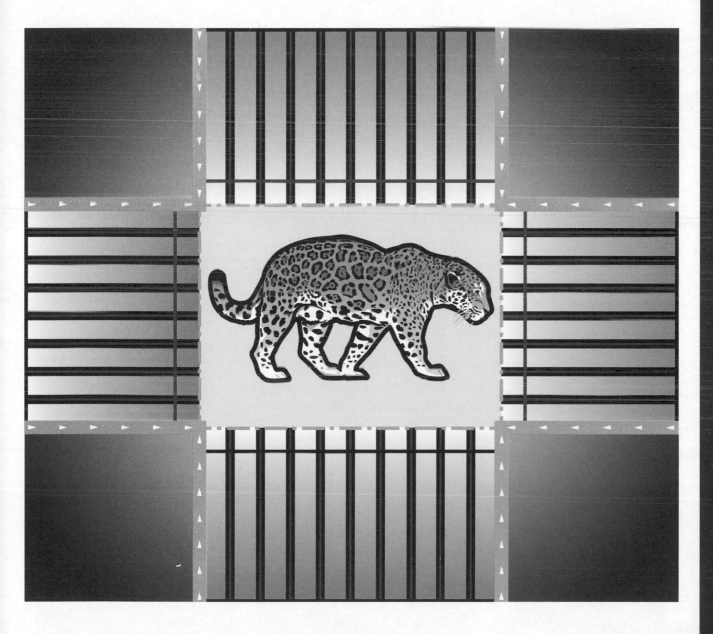

Snake

Cut along the arrows to make a purple snake.
Hang the spiral by a string from the dot in the center.

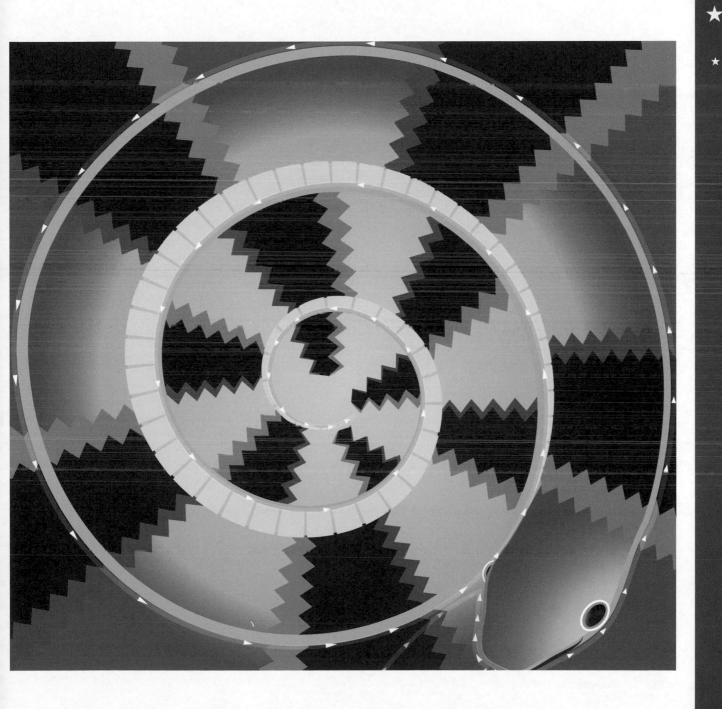

ANSWER KEY

Page 42

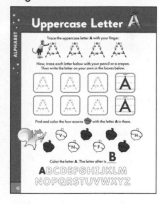

Page 43

Page 44

Page 45

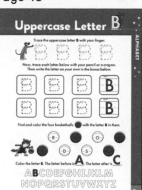

Page 46

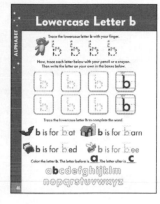

Page 47

Page 48

Page 49

Page 50

Page 51

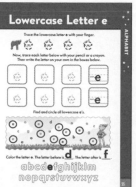

Page 52

Page 53

Page 54

Page 55

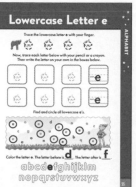

Page 56

Page 57

ANSWER KEY

Page 58

Page 59

Page 60

Page 61

Page 62

Page 63

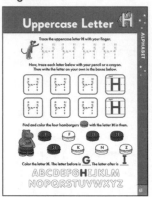

Page 64

Page 65

Page 66

Page 67

Page 68

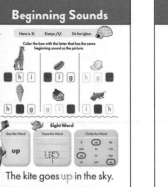

Page 69

Page 70

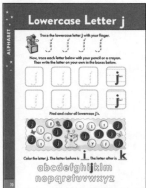

Page 71

Page 72

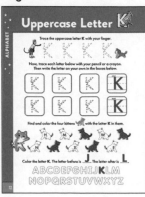

Page 73

ANSWER KEY

Page 74

Page 75

Page 76

Page 77

Page 78

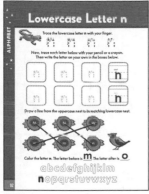

Page 79

Page 80

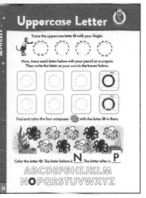

Page 81

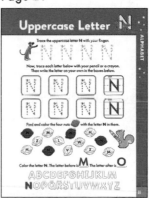

Page 82

Page 83

Page 84

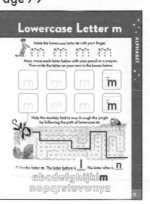

Page 85

Page 86

Page 87

Page 88

Page 89

ANSWER KEY

Page 90

Page 91

Page 92

Page 93

Page 94

Page 95

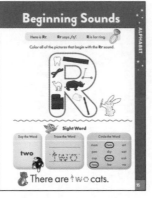

Page 96

Page 97

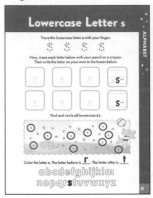

Page 98

Page 99

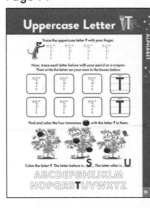

Page 100

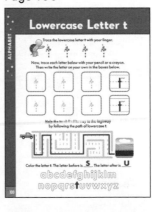

Page 101

Page 102

Page 103

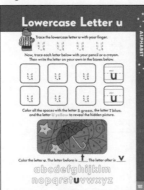

Page 104

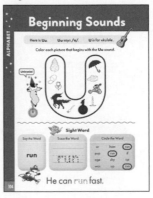

Page 105

ANSWER KEY

Page 106

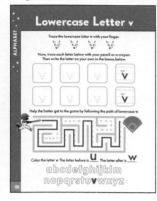

Page 107

Page 108

Page 109

Page 110

Page 111

Page 112

Page 113

Page 114

Page 115

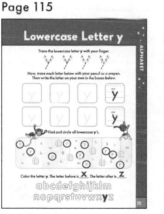

Page 116

Page 117

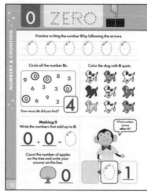

Page 118

Page 119

Page 121

Page 122

ANSWER KEY

Page 123

Page 124

Page 125

Page 126

Page 127

Page 128

Page 129

Page 130

Page 131

Page 132

Page 133

Page 134

Page 137

Page 138

Page 139

Page 140

ANSWER KEY

Page 141

Page 142

Page 143

Page 144

Page 145

Page 146

Page 147

Page 148

Page 151

Page 152

Page 153

Page 154

Page 155

Page 156

Page 157

Page 158

ANSWER KEY

Page 159

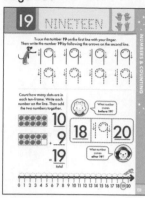

Page 160

Page 161

Page 163

Page 164

Page 165

Page 166

Page 167

Page 168

Page 169

Page 170

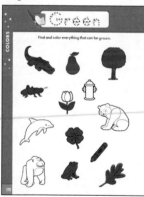

Page 171

Page 172

Page 173

Page 174

Page 175

ANSWER KEY

Page 176

Page 177

Page 178

Page 179

Page 180

Page 181

Page 182

Page 185

Page 186

Page 188

Page 189

Page 191

Page 192

Page 194

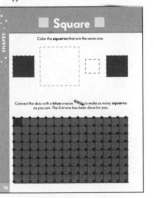

Page 195

Page 197

ANSWER KEY

Page 198

Page 200

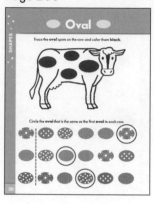

Page 201

Page 203

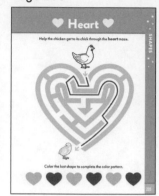

Page 204

Page 206

Page 207

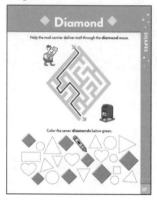

Page 210

Page 213

Page 214

Page 217

Page 218

Page 219

Page 220

Page 221

Page 222

ANSWER KEY

Page 223

Seasons: Fall

Page 224

Seasons

Page 225

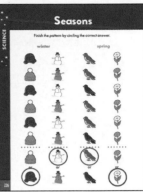

Seasons

Page 226

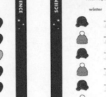

Seasons

Page 227

Is It Hot or Is It Cold?

Page 228

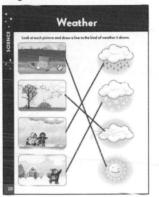

Weather

Page 230

Life Cycle of Plants

Page 231

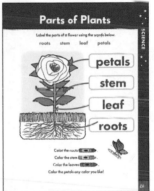

Parts of Plants

Page 232

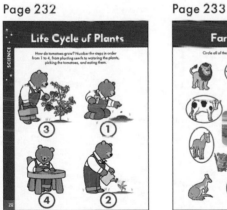

Life Cycle of Plants

Page 233

Farm Animals

Page 234

Ocean Animals

Page 235

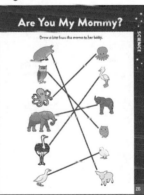

Are You My Mommy?

Page 236

Fly or Swim?

Page 237

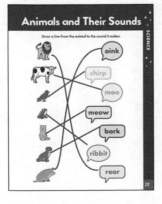

Animals and Their Sounds

Page 238

Animals and Their Homes

Page 240

Same

ANSWER KEY

Page 241

Same

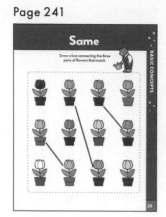

Page 242

Different

Page 243

Different

Page 244

Opposites

Page 245

Opposites

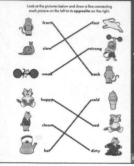

Page 246

Differences

Page 247

Differences

Page 248

What Is Hot?

Page 249

What Is Cold?

Page 250

Directions

Page 251

Directions

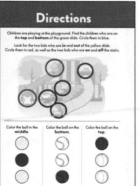
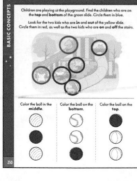

Page 252

Left

Page 253

Right

Page 254

Match the Picture to Its Shape

Page 255

Things That Go Together

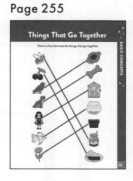

Page 256

Things That Go Together

Page 257

What's Wrong with This Picture?

ANSWER KEY

Page 258
Rhyming
Look at the first picture in each row.
Circle the picture to the right that rhymes with it.

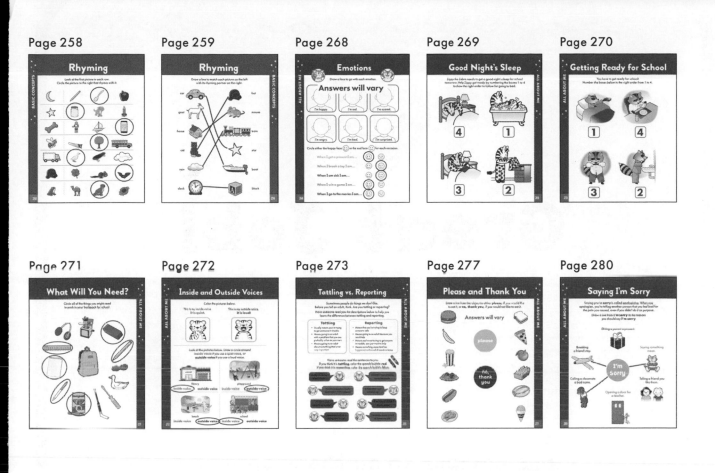

Page 259
Rhyming
Draw a line to match each picture on the left
with its rhyming partner on the right.

Page 268
Emotions
Draw a face to go with each emotion.
Answers will vary

Circle either the happy face or the sad face for each occasion.

When I get a present I am ...
When I break a toy I am ...
When I am sick I am ...
When I win a game I am ...
When I go to the movies I am ...

Page 269
Good Night's Sleep
Zippy the Zebra needs to get a good night's sleep for school tomorrow. Help Zippy get ready by numbering the boxes 1 to 4 to show the right order to follow for going to bed.

Page 270
Getting Ready for School
You have to get ready for school!
Number the boxes below in the right order from 1 to 4.

Page 271
What Will You Need?
Circle all of the things you might need
to pack in your backpack for school.

Page 272
Inside and Outside Voices
Color the pictures below.
This is my inside voice. It is quiet.
This is my outside voice. It is loud!

Look at the pictures below. Draw a circle around inside voice if you use a quiet voice, or outside voice if you use a loud voice.

library — inside voice / outside voice
playground — inside voice / **outside voice**

beach — inside voice / **outside voice**
school — inside voice / outside voice

Page 273
Tattling vs. Reporting
Sometimes people do things we don't like.
Before you tell an adult, think. Are you tattling or reporting?
Have someone read you the descriptions below to help you
learn the difference between tattling and reporting.

Tattling
Reporting

Have someone read the sentences to you.
If you think it's **tattling**, color the speech bubble **red**.
If you think it is reporting, color the speech bubble **blue**.

Page 277
Please and Thank You
Draw a line from the object to either please, if you would like
to eat it, or no, thank you, if you would not like to eat.

Answers will vary

please

no, thank you

Page 280
Saying I'm Sorry
Saying you're sorry is called apologizing. When you
apologize, you're telling another person that you feel bad for
the pain you caused, even if you didn't do it on purpose.
Draw a line from each I'm sorry to the reason
you should say I'm sorry.

Hitting a person on purpose.

Breaking a friend's toy.
Saying something mean.

Calling a classmate a bad name.
I'm Sorry
Telling a friend you like them.

Opening a door for a teacher.

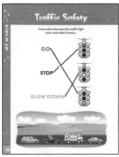

Page 281
Saying Excuse Me
You say **excuse me** in social meaning.
When should you say **excuse me**?
Answer yes or no to the following situations.

When you bump into a teacher?
yes no

When you need to get the librarian's attention?
yes no

When you did not hear or understand what a classmate said?
yes no

When you read a book?
yes **no**

When you burp?
yes no

When you sneeze?
yes no

Page 283
Be Kind to Others
Be kind to others by treating them the way you want to be treated.
Draw a line from each direction to either kind or unkind.

kind

unkind

Asking a classmate to play with you.

Waiting in line to take a turn.

Picking up a book for a friend who dropped it.

Getting mad at a friend.

Not allowing a classmate to play with you.

Letting a friend borrow your crayons.

Page 286
Stop, Look, and Listen
Before we cross any street we have to
stop, look, and listen!

Draw a line from each word to its matching picture.

STOP
LOOK
LISTEN

Page 287
Traffic Lights
The color of a traffic light tells cars what to do. Red means stop, yellow means slow down and look for cars, and green means go.

red
yellow
green

Page 288
Traffic Safety
Draw a line between the traffic light
color and what it means.

GO
STOP
SLOW DOWN

Page 289
Stop Signs
A stop sign is red with white letters.
It has a white border and eight sides.
When you see it on a street, you should stop.
Connect the dots from 1 to 8 to 1 to complete
the stop sign below. Then color it.

STOP

Page 289
Car Safety
Circle the correct way to ride in a car.

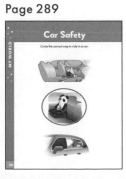

Page 291
Helmet Safety
You always need to wear a helmet when
you're on a bike, a skateboard, or a scooter.

Helmets are important for safety. Draw a line from the boy with
the helmet to the activities where he must wear a helmet.

playing basketball
riding a skateboard
riding in a car
riding a bike

playing hopscotch
going to the dentist
riding a scooter

Page 292
Important People
Circle the people whose job it is to care for others.

Page 293
Workers and Their Tools
Draw a line from each person to the object they use at work.

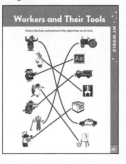

319

Great Job!

_____

name

has completed all the exercises
in this workbook and is ready
for pre-kindergarten.

_____

date